OPERATION 'HUSKY'
The Allied Invasion of Sicily

OPERATION 'HUSKY'

THE ALLIED INVASION OF SICILY

S. W. C. PACK

Introduction by
Vice-Admiral Lord Ashbourne, CB, DSO, JP

HIPPOCRENE
BOOKS, INC

NEW YORK, N.Y.

9 40. 54 2 1

P 12 o

1 0 5 7 0 8

July 1 9 7 8

© S. W. C. Pack 1977

All Rights Reserved

Hippocrene Books, Inc
171 Madison Avenue
New York, N.Y. 10016

Library of Congress Cataloging in Publication Data

Pack, S W C
    Operation 'Husky' : the allied invasion of Sicily.

    Bibliography: p.
    Includes index.
        1. World War, 1939–1945—Campaigns—Italy—Sicily.
2. Operation Husky, 1943.   3. Sicily—History—1870–
    I. Title.
D763.S5P32   940.54'21   77–3075
ISBN 0–88254–440–3

Printed in Great Britain

Contents

Introduction   7
Preface and Acknowledgements   9
Abbreviations   13

1   Grand Strategy   15
2   Initial Plan   27
3   Rejection   33
4   The Invasion Beaches   37
5   Naval Aspect   47
6   Air Aspect   61
7   Western Assault   73
8   Eastern Assault   89
9   Supplementary Roles   119
10   The Struggle for Sicily   135
11   Conclusion   160

Appendix I   175
Chronology of Events
Pre-HUSKY
During HUSKY

Appendix II   178
Ship Losses during Assault

Bibliography   180
Index   181

List of Maps

Map 1   Sicily: highways, roads, rivers and airfields   28–9
Map 2   Operation HUSKY: final plan for assault
         landings, 10 July 1943   38–9
Map 3   Invasion of Sicily: main routes of assault
         convoys to assembly   49
Map 4   Invasion of Sicily: rough routes of Allied
         ground forces   136–7

Introduction

by
Vice-Admiral Lord Ashbourne, CB, DSO, JP

Having taken part in Operation HUSKY, I am honoured and delighted to have been asked by the author to contribute a brief introduction to this, his latest book.

Captain Pack has done it again, and has added yet one more to his already long list of books.

The difficulties of planning Operation HUSKY, with the headquarters of the senior commanders as widely separated as the USA, the UK, Algiers, and Cairo, is well brought out, and under these circumstances it is amazing that such good results were achieved.

There was, as usual, too big a volume of paper churned out and it was difficult to read and absorb all the orders before the operation began. The orders were of course closely related to the latest intelligence, and this latter was continually bringing new and very relevant information to light.

Here I would add a word on the high quality of our own intelligence; gained, as always, from many and varied sources, it found its way into photographs taken by the RAF, into models made by the army, and into beach and foreshore data obtained by naval sources, largely by submarines. One of my biggest thrills was the view from the bridge of my ship at the first light of dawn on D-day. It revealed a view that was exactly as I had expected.

Captain Pack's story brings out so well the vital part played by weather, not only to the operations of naval and air forces, but to the great discomfort of the army in seasickness and difficulty in disembarking in the dark and in many cases in water too deep for comfort or safety. Captain Pack makes it clear, however, that once the word 'go' has been given, it is almost impossible to reverse it and postpone the operation. The risk of chaos is too great, and this was well demonstrated not only in HUSKY but a year later in OVERLORD (the invasion of Normandy).

As the reader will see, Admiral Cunningham sent an inspiring signal to all concerned, at the beginning of the operation. The wording of this was so exactly right and so much to the point that it is worth reading a second (and third) time. In so many words he says that the operation must go on, whatever the cost. How much easier that makes life for subordinate commanders. There can be no doubt left in their minds. However rough the weather, however late the landing, however difficult the navigation, or whatever the enemy opposition, the landing must go on.

Captain Pack has wisely added to his narrative of HUSKY a number of personal experiences from officers and men of all ranks, and this of course adds greatly to the human side of the story. It fills a long-felt gap. The story of HUSKY has been told before, as part of the history of the war as a whole, but I, for one, have never yet come across a book solely on the story of HUSKY; a splendid book that is full of interest and will be enjoyed by all.

ASHBOURNE

Preface and Acknowledgements

The Allied invasion of Sicily, 10 July 1943, was described by Admiral of the Fleet Sir Andrew Cunningham, at that time Commander-in-Chief, Mediterranean, as 'the most momentous enterprise of the war . . . striking for the first time at the enemy in his own land'.

In retrospect it should be realised that the invasion was only first seriously discussed 6 months before it took place; and the final decision was made only 6 weeks before the event. As described in Chapter 1, it will be apparent to the reader that agreement was not easily reached. It may prove helpful to a better understanding of the circumstances leading to Operation HUSKY if reference is made to the Chronology of Events listed in Appendix I.

It is a fact that not only is there a continuing interest in the events of World War II as the years elapse, but a growing interest. In response to an appeal for material I received an almost overwhelming collection of diaries, maps, guides, pamphlets, and 270 individual accounts of experiences from those who participated in HUSKY. Although it is practicable to reproduce only a fraction of these, I wish to express my thanks to all concerned, whether reproduced or not. Their accounts are interesting and valuable in adding realism to the narrative.

We are often accused of studying strategy and tactics that are out of date. Yet we are seldom admonished for repeatedly ignoring the lessons of history that recur with amazing regularity as the years pass.

Weapons and tactics are constantly changing, but strategical factors such as alliances, preparedness, flexibility, mobility, coordination, replenishment bases, the element of surprise, human morale, dedication to service and, above all, the personal touch of the leader, can only be neglected at a nation's peril.

I wish to thank authors, publishers, and copyright holders for the privilege of referring to publications, particularly the military histories, in the Bibliography at the end of this book.

I had the benefit of working with the Combined Chiefs of Staff in Washington during the planning of HUSKY, and although not at sea for the operation, enjoyed the vicarious experience of following the fortunes of well-known ships that had survived those difficult days of 1940–1, before the United States joined the British Commonwealth as a great and indispensable ally.

I am very grateful to those who provided me with photographs for reproduction, and also to Messrs Hine and Squires of the Imperial War Museum for assistance. My thanks are due also to Vice-Admiral Lord Ashbourne, CB, DSO, Senior Naval Officer (landing) at BARK East during the assault, for his great kindness in reading my manuscript and for writing such a helpful introduction.

Above all I owe the greatest thanks to my wife for her endless encouragement and help.

Dartmouth
Devon   S. W. C. PACK

The author is greatly indebted to the following for permission to reproduce photographs as shown in the captions: J. Bayley (JB); Surgeon Captain Gartside (SCG); Imperial War Museum (IWM); C. H. W. Pitt (CHWP); D. L. C. Price (DLCP); Lieut-Cdr L. J. Smith (LJS); US Navy (USN)

Dedicated to the memory of
Captain A. A. Havers, OBE, DSC, RN
and in memory of all who took part in
Operation 'Husky'

Abbreviations

AA	Anti-aircraft
AOC	Air Officer Commanding
A/S	Anti-submarine
BAD	British Admiralty Delegation
BJCOS	British Joint Chiefs of Staff
BJSM	British Joint Staff Mission
C47	Transport aircraft
CAS	Chief of the Air Staff
CCO	Chief of Combined Operations
CCS	Combined Chiefs of Staff
CIGS	Chief of the Imperial General Staff
CMB	Coastal Motor Boat
CNS	Chief of the Naval Staff
COS	Chief of Staff; Chiefs of Staff
C-in-C	Commander-in-Chief
CO	Commanding Officer
CTF	Commander Task Force
DUKW	Amphibious vehicle
ENTF	Eastern Naval Task Force
ETF	Eastern Task Force
FW190	Focke-Wulf fighter
HDML	Harbour Defence Motor Launch
Ju87	Junkers single seat bomber
Ju88	Junkers medium bomber
LCA	Landing Craft Assault
LCF	Landing Craft Flak
LCI	Landing Craft Infantry
LCT	Landing Craft Tank
LSI	Landing Ship Infantry
LST	Landing Ship Tank
Me109	Messerschmitt fighter
MGB	Motor Gun Boat

See pp. 44–5, for further details of landing craft and landing ships

M/S	Minesweeper
MTB	Motor Torpedo Boat
S/M	Submarine
SNOL	Senior Naval Officer Landing
USAF	US Air Force (originally USAAF signifying US Army Air Force)
USJCOS	US Joint Chiefs of Staff
WNTF	Western Naval Task Force
WTF	Western Task Force

14

1 Grand Strategy

It was on 14 January 1943 that Roosevelt, the President of the United States of America, met Churchill, the Prime Minister of Great Britain, in a conference at Casablanca. It will be recalled that the Allied landings on the north-west African coast on 8 November 1942 had been successful, as also had been General Montgomery's breakthrough with the Eighth Army at El Alamein on 7 November 1942.

The purpose of the Casablanca Conference was to discuss the next Allied step in grand strategy, to be undertaken as soon as Axis forces had been driven out of North Africa. The latter attainment, somewhat optimistically, was regarded at that time as being only a matter of 2–3 months away.

American and British Chiefs of Staff had been summoned to attend the Casablanca Conference. It may be helpful here to refer individually to those senior military leaders who constituted vitally important committees from 1942 onwards. It is also necessary to elaborate the significance of the two words 'combined' and 'joint'. A 'combined' committee was one in which officers of two or more nations served together: an Allied committee as distinct from a national. A 'joint' committee, on the other hand, indicated collaboration and discussion between the military, naval, and air services of one nation. Serving in Washington, for example, was the joint committee of the American Chiefs of Staff, composed of General Marshall (Army), Admiral King (Navy), and General Arnold (Air Force). This was comparable with the joint committee of the heads of British services serving in London, composed of Admiral Pound, General Brooke, and Air Chief Marshal Portal. This joint committee of the British chiefs of staff had its permanent representation in Washington in the British Joint Staff Mission (BJSM), of which Field Marshal Sir John Dill was head. The combination of the American chiefs of staff and the BJSM in Washington formed what was known as the Combined Chiefs of Staff Committee (CCS), and met regularly in Washington to agree on the strategic direction of Allied forces and the allocation of manpower, munitions, and shipping. Their function was not only advisory in making agreed recommendations to Roosevelt and Churchill, but was also executive as soon as final agreements had been reached.

In March 1942 the British Chiefs of Staff Committee in London had received an additional member in the person of Lord Louis Mountbatten. As Chief of Combined Operations (CCO), with the acting rank of vice-admiral, lieutenant-general, and air marshal, he was granted full membership. Combined operations, better known as amphibious warfare, had received inadequate recognition during the years between the wars and in the early period of the war, largely owing to lack of coordination between the armed forces. Under Mount-batten's skilful and vigorous direction vast strides were now being made in the study and practice of amphibious operations, assisted by moral and material support that followed America's entry into the war. It should be remembered, however, that America had not been ready for war, and when she entered at the time of Pearl Harbour, had no specific plan. The enemy was successful almost everywhere at that time, and America's natural decision was to appropriate for herself much of the war material previously allocated to Britain. The growing success of U-boat warfare in 1942 accentuated an increasing shortage of Allied shipping, and the vital need to build new ships seriously interfered with the requirement for a massive supply of assault landing craft for amphibious operations. Operation TORCH, the Allied amphibious assault on North

Africa, had revealed the growing need for landing craft, not only those required for the next operation but the craft required for the considerable personnel training which it was necessary to develop.

At the time of the Casablanca Conference, January 1943, the Allies were virtually split in their strategic views. Though Stalin was not represented at the conference, it was uppermost in most minds that he had forcefully demanded an early offensive by America and Britain that would relieve the critical situation on the Russian front.

The British team at Casablanca were keen on what became known as the Mediterranean strategy, claiming that the prizes would be the reopening of the short-sea route, the reduction of German air power in the Mediterranean, and the early

CCS at Casablanca January 1943: on left, *King, Marshall, Arnold (hidden);* (r to l) *Dill, Portal, Brooke, Pound, Mountbatten* (IWM)

elimination of Italy from the war. They admitted that this would be at the expense of ROUND-UP, the long proposed direct attack across the English Channel which, because of the continued shortage of shipping and therefore the slow build-up of US troops in Britain, might not be feasible until 1944. The suggestion by the British was that either Sicily or Sardinia should be seized, and the war carried into the Balkans in order to deny oil and minerals to the Germans. Consideration of a likely date for such operations was, however, not practicable before a favourable termination of the existing Tunisian campaign could be seen to be near. Nevertheless planning for Operation HUSKY (the capture of Sicily) was pursued in London, while planning for Operation BRIM-STONE (the capture of Sardinia) was undertaken at General Eisenhower's Allied Force Headquarters in Algiers, until such time as a decision could be reached as to where to strike next.

At Casablanca there were, in addition to the Chiefs of Staff Committees, Field Marshal Dill of the BJSM, with members of his mission, and the principal members of the British Joint Planning Staff, who were very strongly in favour of the Mediterranean strategy, now to be proposed by the British delegates. On the American side of the discussion there was not as yet any agreed or positive plan, although General Marshall made it clear that he had strong reservations about continuing operations in the Mediterranean while the threat of a German thrust southward through Spain existed. He wished the main effort against Germany to be made in 1943 across the English Channel – Operation ROUND-UP – despite the opinion of American and British planners that such an operation as early as 1943 could not be assured of success. Already he had been advised by General Eisenhower, on the basis of experience in the North Africa landings, that the number of landing craft required for a main offensive across the English Channel would be twice what had been originally estimated. Admiral King, whose chief concern at that moment lay in the Pacific, appeared to have an open mind about the Mediterranean strategy, whereas General Arnold, who appreciated in particular the great advantage of acquiring air bases in the Mediterranean, was a supporter. Whatever was to be decided, it was clear that the invasion of Sicily would be an undertaking of the first magnitude.

On the British side General Brooke described cogently the possibly disastrous results for ROUND-UP because of the critical shortage of shipping that had arisen, a feature which could strangle a large offensive across the English Channel, especially if the Allies were unable to neutralise the U-boat menace. The main German attack on Russia had failed, and the Germans were already on the defensive both in Russia and in North Africa, faced with a growing shortage of oil and manpower. The best way to help the Russians at that moment was to attack Germany, not in north-west Europe, where her good east-west communications would be in her favour, but in the Mediterranean where, in expectation of possible attack in the Balkans, Sicily, Sardinia, or Corsica, she would have to fight with her forces widely dispersed. The Allies might compel Italy to leave the war, and thus encourage Turkey to come in, with the provision of bases for future attacks, and the offer of easy access to Russia through the Black Sea. Admiral Pound and Air Chief Marshal Portal supported these views, the former emphasising also the need for escort vessels and long-range aircraft in the war against U-boats, and the latter urging that with growing Allied air superiority there should be an increasing onslaught on German air power.

In the course of further discussions during the next 5 days of the Casablanca Conference the various viewpoints were reconciled, and an agreement reached. The CCS met Roosevelt and Churchill on the afternoon of 18 January 1943, and General Marshall summarised the agreed points, which now required confirmation. He was satisfied as to the need for an invasion of Sicily at the earliest moment feasible, and no longer concerned that the Allies might be getting entangled in fruitless operations in the Mediterranean at the expense of war against Japan. It was quite understood that Germany must be defeated while Japan was being brought to a standstill. The crucial operation of ROUND-UP across the English Channel must be deferred until 1944. The relevant points concerning the immediate future conduct of the war were as follows:

1 The occupation of Sicily, thus strengthening the Mediterranean lines of communication and intensifying pressure on Italy;
2 The enlistment of Turkey if possible;
3 The assembly of the strongest forces ready for entry into Europe at the most suitable moment.

The Americans showed sympathy with Churchill's determination to continue to succour the Russians, and offered material help in the matter of escort ships, especially for the defeat of the U-boat. Nearly 8 million tons of Allied shipping had been sunk in 1942. Perhaps one of the most significant declarations made at Casablanca was the requirement for *unconditional* surrender of the enemy.

Although the British representatives had pressed hard for the Mediterranean strategy, it was not until the last days of the Conference that agreement was reached as between Operation BRIMSTONE (Sardinia) and Operation HUSKY (Sicily). The Americans were content to leave the choice to the British. Mountbatten was for Sardinia on the grounds that it could be taken more rapidly and would entail a smaller amphibious force. He was supported in this choice by Admiral of the Fleet Sir Andrew Cunningham, the Allied Naval Commander in the Mediterranean. Pound, Brooke, and Portal (especially the latter) favoured Sicily, however, on the basis that possession of the Sicilian airfields would give effective control of the straits between Tunisia and Sicily.

Eventually the decision hardened towards Sicily, perhaps because it was felt that it was a more worthwhile venture, and with its endless possibilities would satisfy the Russian demand for a second front more effectively than the capture of Sardinia. The main problem was 'How soon can it take place?' Some 3,000 ships and craft were needed, plus detailed reconnaissance, and huge quantities of men, vehicles, tanks, guns, equipment, food, and water; and in the meantime Axis forces in North Africa were putting up a fierce defence, helped greatly by the atrocious weather and waterlogged roads. Despite these disadvantageous conditions for the Allied forces, Churchill would brook no delay, and by his insistence it was resolved that planning should begin at once and HUSKY would be launched on 10 July 1943 at a suitable state of the moon, which would ensure darkness for 4 hours from the time of moonset at 12.31am to first light at 4.39am.

As soon as the President and the Prime Minister had approved the proposals of the CCS at the final plenary session of the Casablanca Conference, a directive was issued to General Eisenhower at Algiers, with an outline plan indicating invasion of Sicily by two forces – a Western Task Force and an Eastern Task Force. Commands for this operation, designated HUSKY, were nominated as follows:

C-in-C, later known as Supreme Commander: General Eisenhower.
Deputy C-in-C, later known as Deputy Supreme Commander: General Alexander.
Allied Naval Commander: Admiral of the Fleet, Sir Andrew Cunningham. (This officer, promoted Admiral of the Fleet on 21 January 1943, should not be confused with Admiral Sir John Cunningham, C-in-C Levant. References to Cunningham below concern Andrew, later Viscount, Cunningham, unless specifically stated otherwise.)
Allied Air Commander: Air Chief Marshal Tedder.

As commander of the Eighteenth Army Group, Alexander was at this time fully occupied in fighting the Tunisian campaign.

No less occupied were Cunningham and Tedder. Cunningham commanded the western approaches to Gibraltar and also the whole of the Mediterranean westward of a line through Corfu and Benghazi, an area which covered all the approaches to Sicily. Tedder had already become an expert in the Western Desert in combining both air and surface operations, and in providing the army with close tactical air support. It is interesting to hark back to the attitude of a group of touring American senators who were anxious to be assured that Eisenhower really had the top job. They put the question to Secretary Stimson: 'If Cunningham commands the naval forces, Tedder the air forces, and Alexander the ground forces, what in hell does Eisenhower command?' The obvious answer was, 'He commands Cunningham, Tedder, and Alexander', which seemed to satisfy their concern. Eisenhower for his part, weighed down by every conceivable problem, was happy to leave the details of planning to his triumvirate and their deputies, and had the greatest confidence in them. There was great mutual respect and admiration.

On 11 February Eisenhower nominated the principal subordinate commanders for the land, sea, and air commands of the two task forces to be mounted for HUSKY:

Western Task Force
Lt-General George Patton, to be Commander US Seventh Army.
Vice-Admiral Henry Hewitt, USN.
Colonel T. J. Hickey, USAAF.
Eastern Task Force
Lt-General Sir Bernard Montgomery, Commander British Eighth Army.
Admiral Sir Bertram Ramsay, Deputy Naval Commander Allied Expeditionary Force.
Air Vice-Marshal Broadhurst, Commander Western Desert Air Force.

Of the above principal subordinate commanders, Montgomery had already taken Tripoli on 23 January 1943 and was pushing on westward to link with the First and Seventh Armies, which were heavily engaged in Tunisia. Because Rommel was putting up such a strong defence in his withdrawal from the Western Desert it would be early May before all Axis forces, by then under General von Arnim, made their final surrender to Alexander in Tunisia.

In the meantime, under great secrecy, planning went ahead in order to arrange for the necessary number of ships to take the requisite troops and equipment to the various beaches that were to be selected for the assault, while in accordance with an exceedingly complex programme, yet to be produced, every man would arrive at the appropriate moment from distant, widely dispersed points. Though the first ships of the assault forces would all reach the assault points on D-day, their routes and progress would have to be calculated so that the ships would not remain in a great concentration for longer than could be avoided. The element of surprise would have to be sustained; and, to support this, cover plans were necessary. Follow-up ships would have to arrive at the assault points as soon as the first-comers departed after unloading.

Meanwhile the fierce fighting in Tunisia had to continue, still under Eisenhower's supreme command; and at the same time readiness must be maintained to counter any Axis threat that might develop in the Iberian peninsula and Spanish Morocco. Since ships and troops for HUSKY would have to assemble from such widely dispersed places as the United States, the United Kingdom, the Middle East, and North Africa, many headquarters would be concerned in the planning, the main centres being London, Washington, Algiers, and Cairo.

In the beginning it was necessary to assess the strength of enemy forces in aircraft, ships, and troops in the island of Sicily, with due regard to the ease with which Axis reserves could be transferred from the mainland of Italy across the narrow Straits of Messina – the latter a simple matter compared with the difficulties of landing Allied troops across the sandy beaches in the south of Sicily. It was estimated at first that there were nine Italian divisions and one German division, probably more, already in Sicily. The disposition of Axis divisions, and their movements, were revealed to a large extent by virtue of Allied knowledge of the German ULTRA cipher. There were also many airfields, as well as minefields and gun batteries. The Italian naval force was formidable in numbers but, to reduce the risk of damage from air attack, was dispersed in various ports. Shortage of oil fuel, and the policy of keeping a fleet in being, restricted the number of occasions of its appearance at sea. Nevertheless an Allied attack on the homeland might well spur the Italians to a fleet offensive.

The most critical problem for the Allies was the shortage of landing craft, a problem made more critical by the time factor and the requirement to assemble men and material in the right number at the right place, as well as to obtain practice in handling the craft. Besides the continuing threat to Allied shipping by Axis aircraft based on Sardinia, Sicily, and Crete, Axis submarines were still a potential danger, especially those German U-boats that had been able to get through the Straits of Gibraltar to attack Allied and neutral shipping routes in the Mediterranean. By the second half of 1943, however, the U-boat threat was markedly declining.

More than 300 miles of the coastline of Sicily had to be photographed and examined. Also the layout of the Sicilian airports was a highly important factor in Allied planning. There were three main groups, all within 15 miles of the coast: the Gerbini group near Catania in the east; the Ponte Olivo group near Gela in the south; and the Castelvetrano group near Palermo in the west. The Germans were shortly to reinforce their air squadrons in the Tyrrhenian, Ionian, and Aegean seas at the expense of other places, a token of the success of the deceptive measures used by the Allies to lead the Germans to expect the next offensive almost anywhere.

Hitler bids Mussolini farewell, April 1943 (IWM)

The deception plans were remarkably ingenious, not the least being those concerned with the invention of 'The Man Who Never Was'. A book written by Ewen Montagu describes the scheme. This was Operation MINCEMEAT, in which a dead body in British uniform was to be washed ashore in Spain as an apparent victim of an aircraft crash. Papers in a briefcase included a letter to Alexander indicating that the objective for Operation HUSKY was to be Greece. There was to be a further operation, according to the letter, named BRIM-STONE, objective unspecified, which was to be 'covered' by making Sicily appear to be the destination. Realism was to be added to this by making the timing of assault convoys fit in with this picture, with apparent threats being made also at Crete, Sardinia, Corsica, and the Peloponessus.

On 14 May 1943 the Prime Minister, then in Washington,

received the following telegram: 'MINCEMEAT swallowed rod, line, and sinker by right people and they look like acting on it.'

The deception bolstered the German High Command's assumption that the Balkans would be the objective for the next attack.

2 Initial Plan

In forming the outline for the invasion the planners were very much aware of important strategic considerations, which are best appreciated if we refer to Map 1. Sicily is shaped like a triangle whose base, the eastern coast, is about 120 miles long. The two sides are the northern coast and the southern coast, each of which is 175 miles long. The island is separated from the Italian mainland by the Straits of Messina which are barely 2 miles in width, and are well provided with train-ferries. Possession of Messina was therefore a great strategic advantage, and in the hands of the Axis powers would offer them great facility for bringing in reinforcements at short notice. But whereas the southern end of Sicily was only 55 miles north of Malta, where Allied air strength was now considerable, Messina was 150 miles from Malta, and therefore beyond the range of Allied single-seater fighter aircraft. This fact ruled out the possibility of a direct assault at Messina.

For the same reason, and because of the presence of known coast defences, a direct assault on the big port of Palermo was impracticable. Nevertheless as the largest port in Sicily, after Messina, and in view of its remoteness from Messina, the early capture of Palermo was regarded as indispensable for maintenance and build-up of Allied strength. The assault forces for this purpose would be required to land on the nearest suitable beaches to the port; these were the parts of the coast that lay between Sciacca and Mazzara, 45 miles south-westward of Palermo and close enough to Allied air bases in Tunisia to enjoy fighter cover.

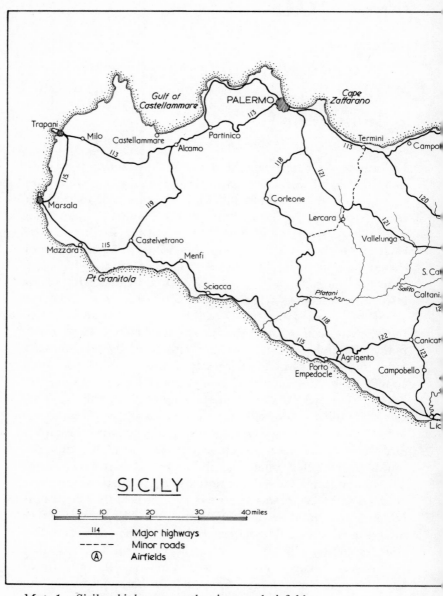

Map 1   Sicily: highways, roads, rivers and airfields

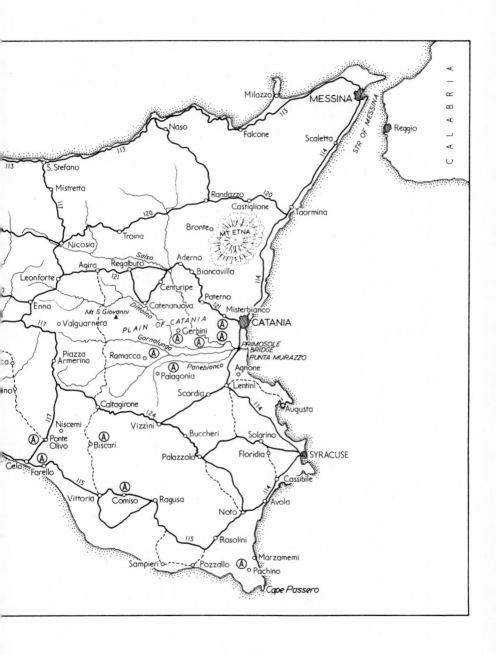

Another indispensable objective was the port of Catania on the east coast, next in size to Palermo, whose capture would permit the maintenance of two divisions and associated air forces, with increasing build-up as time elapsed. A direct assault on Catania was impracticable, however, until shore and coastal batteries could be neutralised by assault parties landing over the beaches, supported by bombardment from Allied warships.

More than 300 miles of coastline had to be surveyed, a difficult and dangerous task necessitating accurate photography and reconnaissance, and skilful reproduction. The sea approaches to the beaches had to give sea-room free from hazards, the coastline had to be instantly recognisable, and such matters as stream, swell, and surf had to be depicted on map sections. Equally important was the nature of the exit inland from the beaches offered to men, vehicles, tanks, and guns as they moved towards their various objectives. A good beach for landing could be nullified if the exit was blocked by cliffs. Surveys showed that Sicily did not offer a wide choice of landing places, only thirty-two or so main beaches being listed as possible for military purposes.

With these facts in mind the planners decided that, in order to capture the island, the invaders would have to take Palermo in the north-west and Catania in the east almost simultaneously at an early date. Palermo was to be the American objective and Catania the British. Each force was to land over beaches where continuous air cover could be provided. Such beaches (for Palermo) lay between Sciacca and Mazzara on the south-west coast, and (for Catania) between Gela in the south and Syracuse in the south-east. The troops were to seize adjacent airfields early on, and then, under the newly provided air cover based on the captured airfields, press on to take the major ports of Palermo and Catania, through which supplies and reinforcements would be brought in at an increasing rate as communications developed.

As remarked above, the landing beaches on the east coast

south of Syracuse, and also those in the vicinity of Sciacca, were within range of Allied fighter cover based on Malta and Tunisia. But the Sciacca beach and the 100-mile length of coastline south of Syracuse would be vulnerable to nearby hostile airfields, of which the main groups were at Gerbini, Comiso, Ponte Olivo, Castelvetrano, Milo, and Palermo. These would have to be reduced before the operation could begin, and plans for this would be made by the Mediterranean Air Command. The outline scheme envisaged the dropping of British parachute brigades to help in the capture of the airfields, these drops being coordinated with the landing assaults, which might themselves be subjected to severe bombing. This was at a time when Allied air policy seemed to have a greater regard for strategic bombing than for the immediate support of tactical movements in an assault in which communications and coordination between services might prove difficult. The air commanders were justifiably more concerned with the necessity of taking local airfields and establishing air bases as quickly as possible than with the difficult and uncertain task of providing support for troops and equipment landing over the beaches. It was Tedder who was to gain the reputation for skilfully combining air and surface operations and providing the army with close tactical support. Certainly the air plan came in for much criticism, which will be mentioned later.

Though fighting his own battle against Axis troops in Tunisia, Alexander was, as Eisenhower's deputy, responsible for the planning of HUSKY. On 28 February 1943 his chief of staff, Major-General Gairdner, flew from Algiers to see him at his Eighteenth Army Group headquarters in Tunisia, a flight of 500 miles. Also busy fighting in North Africa were Patton and Montgomery who, as the respective generals to take command of the Seventh and Eighth Armies, had their planning headquarters at Casablanca and Cairo respectively. Also at the headquarters at Cairo were Admiral Ramsay and Montgomery's deputy, Lieutenant-General Dempsey. Also based in Cairo were the three British Commanders-in-Chief Middle

East – navy, army, and air – who, although not directly appointed to the HUSKY project, had considerable responsibility concerning the arrival and assembly of troops, ships, and aircraft arriving in the Mediterranean by the long route round the Cape of Good Hope; and also for the amphibious training schemes necessary before a combined assault could take place. The wide dispersion of these headquarters restricted discussion, and were to lead to difficulties in resolving the different opinions about the HUSKY plan, which at one moment became what Cunningham was to refer to as a deadlock.

When Gairdner visited Alexander in late February 1943, it was already obvious that the basic framework of the original plan suffered from certain defects. Alexander made some improvements, suggesting that both the Western and Eastern Task Forces might be concentrated against the south-east corner of Sicily rather than split up with vast distances between them. He wished to have an adequate reserve. To ensure surprise it was required that the first landings should be made in darkness. It was also still current doctrine that there should be no naval gunfire support during the dark hours for fear of injuring the assaulting troops. In addition preliminary bombardment was deprecated because of its prejudicial effect on the surprise factor, a doctrine soon to be discredited. The new plan made airborne operations a big feature, the main role of the airborne troops being to support the assaulting troops by neutralising shore defences.

The improved plan was recommended by the principal commanders – Alexander, Cunningham, and Tedder – and approved in principle by Eisenhower at a meeting on 13 March. But no word about the plan had yet come from Montgomery, who at that time had just fought the Battle of Medenine, and was preparing for an Eighth Army offensive against the Mareth line.

3 Rejection

Although agreement of the Initial Plan had been reached in principle by Eisenhower, Alexander, Cunningham, and Tedder on 13 March, there had been limited opportunity for either Patton or Montgomery, the nominated army task force commanders, to represent their views. According to Morison (the US Naval Historian), Patton, when urged to protest, is reputed to have said: 'I've been in this Army for thirty years, and when my superior gives me an order I say "Yes, Sir!", and then do my goddamndest to carry it out.' Montgomery on the other hand was critical. He disliked the plan so much when visited on 18 March in Tripoli by Lieutenant-General Dempsey, his deputy, that in spite of his preoccupation with the Mareth offensive, he asked Dempsey and Admiral Ramsay to lodge his objections with Alexander, then in Algiers. In a message to Alexander, late in March, Montgomery said that the outline plan 'breaks every commonsense rule of practical battle-fighting and is completely theoretical. It has no hope of success and should be completely recast.' This amounted to a sudden and stunning rejection.

Montgomery's view was that by landing at widely separated places with troops dispersed over some 100 miles of beaches the Allies would lay themselves open to defeat in detail. The capture of the eastern ports of Syracuse, Augusta, and Catania was vital to provide for maintenance after the landings, and it was therefore necessary to have greater concentration at Avola, 15 miles south of Syracuse, on the first day, to the extent of an extra division. Since it was unlikely that an extra division and all the necessary ships and craft would be available it looked as though the concentration at Avola could be attained only at the expense of the 50 miles of beaches on the south coast between Pachino and Gela. This reduction of frontage would militate against the prospect of taking the airfields in the vicinity of Comiso, Ponte Olivo, and Gela.

Tedder demurred at this, saying, 'I can understand that the Eastern Task Force commander Montgomery rightly regards the capture of the eastern ports as vital and that he considers an extra division essential for this purpose, but air superiority is equally vital and must have priority. Unless air superiority is maintained over the landings during the first forty-eight hours, the landings themselves may fail.' Admiral Cunningham, who had sad memories of Axis air superiority in the Mediterranean during 1941 and 1942, supported Tedder's view.

Alexander then suggested to Eisenhower that the proposed American landing at Sciacca should be abandoned. The American division earmarked for that assault could instead land at Gela in the place of the British division which Montgomery wished to add to the forces assaulting the Avola beaches in the south-east. This would, however, entail a postponement of two days for the landings of the American divisions, whose early objective was to be the vital port of Palermo. It would mean that much of Patton's Western Task Force would have to hang about for an indefinite period waiting for Montgomery's Eastern Task Force to attain its primary objectives. And during this time the enemy could concentrate at will against the Eastern Task Force.

These suggestions therefore found no support either in Algiers, Washington, or London. It was discovered, however, that an extra division and the necessary landing craft could be made available, provided that all idea of a 1943 invasion of France was immediately abandoned. Hence, on 10 April, Eisenhower approved a new plan submitted by Alexander and Montgomery on 5 April, which added a British division to the Eastern Task Force, which would then comprise:

1 Two divisions to land at Avola;
2 A brigade to land at Pachino;
3 One division to land at Pozzallo;
4 One division to land at Gela.

It would be tedious to describe all the further discussions and changes of mind, which in restrospect appear so incredible. It should be remembered that this was a period when lessons were being learned yearly, monthly, and even daily, and the undertaking of a gigantic amphibious invasion of enemy territory, in the face perhaps of fierce and concentrated counter-attacks, was a matter that could be argued upon only after the most profound consideration.

At this stage Eisenhower applied a firm hand and called for a further meeting on 2 May. This meeting was a main turning point in planning, with Montgomery producing an entirely new plan that he presented with great conviction, and which secured Eisenhower's support. The plan was explained by Montgomery on 2–3 May at Algiers on behalf of Alexander, who had been grounded by the bad weather in Tunisia. Cunningham and Tedder were present with Eisenhower. The gist of the new plan was that the American attack in the Palermo area should be abandoned and there should be one concentrated punch, American and British, in the south-east of the island. This was a good plan from the army point of view because it avoided dispersion. Cunningham and Tedder still had misgivings at the prospect of so many airfields being left in enemy hands. Cunningham's view was that the Allies' greatest asset – that of the ability to assault the island in numerous places at will with the backing of naval superiority – was being surrendered.

The 3 May plan was finally endorsed by the CCS on 13 May. A few days earlier Axis forces of about a quarter of a million had collapsed and surrendered to Alexander in Tunisia.

Cunningham was not in favour of the new scheme, but promised loyal support for it. His chief of staff records that the general belief in Algiers was that the first plan (Palermo and Catania) would have progressed just as well, and if accepted in the beginning could have been implemented earlier, with adequate preparations and less difficulty over the beach landings. Cunningham writes:

> It has to be realised that any amphibious operation is merely the opening under particular circumstance, of a primarily Army battle. It is the function of the Navy and the Air to help the Army to establish a base on the hostile coast from which the military tactical battle must be developed to gain the final object. At last we had the broad outline of a plan upon which to base our detailed organisation and arrangements. D day for the landing in Sicily was timed for a bare two months ahead.

4 The Invasion Beaches

As soon as the 3 May plan was approved, work began on the details. There had been persistent pressure from Churchill for the proposed date of the invasion to be advanced, but the delay in producing a plan that was acceptable had put this out of the question, and it was confirmed that D-day should be 10 July as originally planned, with the moon at first quarter. With H-hour fixed at 2.45am for the first landings on 10 July there would be no moonlight during the hazardous final approach of the seaborne assaulting troops, since moonset would occur a good 2 hours before this time. This was favourable to the seaborne troops, who wished to land under cover of darkness. The airborne troops, who were to be carried in gliders towed by aircraft and then released for the purpose of capturing important strategic points, were to land 6 minutes after midnight so as to have the benefit of almost half an hour of moonlight in which to develop an attack before the moon set. This was little more than a compromise, which did not serve all requirements.

In order to get some idea of the magnitude of the task of landing two armies in the south-east corner of Sicily the reader is referred to Map 2. It will add to the interest of complex moves which are described later if the reader familiarises himself with the various landing places on the map and the particular force associated with each. Working from left to right we deal first with the 35 miles of coastline, from the small port of Licata to Cape Scaramia.

Patton's Seventh Army was to land along this stretch,

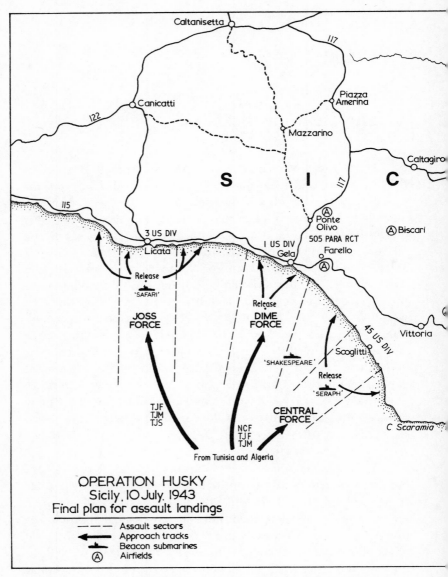

Map 2   *Operation HUSKY: final plan for assault landings,*
10 July 1943

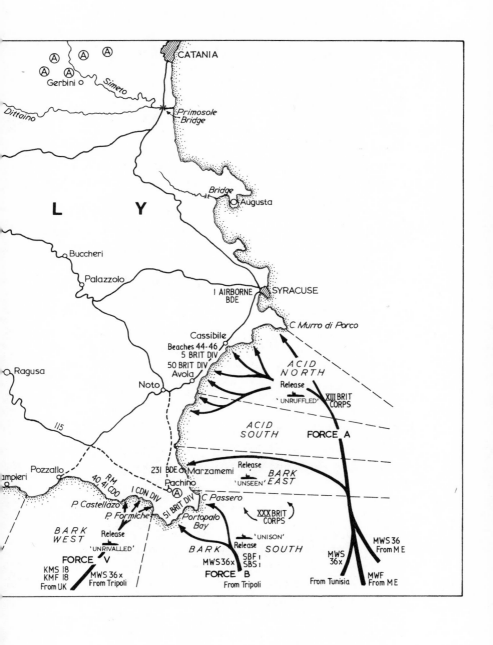

safeguarding the left flank of Montgomery's Eighth Army, and meanwhile advancing northward and to the north-east to establish contact with the Eighth Army in the Ragusa area. The embarkation point and objective of the various formations were to be as follows:

1 3 US Division (Major-Gen Truscott), from Bizerta, to land along a 5-mile stretch each side of Licata, which was to be captured together with Licata airfield and consolidated as a local bridgehead; sector JOSS.

2 1 US Division (Major-Gen Allen), from Algiers and Tunis (together with 505 Parachute Regimental Combat Team), to land at Gela and capture the local and Ponte Olivo airfields; sector DIME.

3 45 US Division (Major-Gen Middleton), from United States, then Oran, to land along a 15-mile stretch near Scoglitti, and to capture airfields at Comiso and Biscari; sector CENT.

4 2 US Armoured Division (Major-Gen Gaffey); floating reserve, except for an armoured combat and a regimental combat team attached to 1 US Division.

9 US Division (Major-Gen Eddy) in reserve.

We now continue left to right around the Pachino peninsula to the east coast where XXX Corps and XIII Corps of Montgomery's Eighth Army were to land on the right flank of Patton's Seventh Army as follows:

XXX Corps (Lt-Gen Leese)

1 1 Canadian Division (Major-Gen Simonds), from UK, to land on the Pachino peninsula between Punta Castellazo and Punta di Formiche, with the task of capturing Pachino airfield and advancing towards Ragusa; sector BARK West.

2 51 Division (Major-Gen Wimberley), from Sousse, Sfax, and Malta, to land at tip of Pachino peninsula to capture Pachino and to consolidate bridgehead; sector BARK South.

3 231 Infantry Brigade (Brig Urquhart), from Suez, to land at Marzamemi to consolidate Pachino bridgehead; sector BARK East.

XIII Corps (Lt-Gen Dempsey)

4 50 Division (Major-Gen Kirkman), from Suez, to land at Avola to consolidate local bridgehead, to protect left flank of XIII Corps, and later, with 5 Division and 1 Airborne Division to capture Augusta and Catania; (ACID South).

5 5 Division (Major-Gen Berney-Ficklin), from Suez, to land at Cassibile, to consolidate local bridgehead, capture Syracuse, and later, in conjunction with 1 Airborne Division to capture Augusta and Catania; (ACID North).

6 1 Air Landing Brigade, from Tunisia, to capture Grande bridge over the River Anapo near Syracuse.

7 2 Parachute Brigade, to capture bridge crossing River Mulinello near Augusta.

8 1 Parachute Brigade, to capture intact Primosole bridge across the River Simeto, to be coordinated with advance of XIII Corps on Catania.

9 78 Division (Major-Gen Evelegh), in reserve.

All the landings except those of 51 Highland and 3 US Divisions were 'Ship to Shore', where men and material were carried in ships to the assault areas and then transferred to landing craft for the final run to the beaches. The landings of 51 Highland and 3 US Divisions were in accordance with a new time-saving plan called 'Shore to Shore', whereby the men and much of the material were carried in the craft that would run them on to the beaches. Many of the landing craft would be transported vast distances in those landing ships, which were capable of carrying them and hoisting them in and out. The shore to shore craft would have to cover a fair distance fully laden, ready for disembarkation at the beaches.

The precise location of beaches was an important factor and, for this, seven submarines were to be stationed at selected

With Churchill at Algiers, June 1943: (l to r) *Eden, Brooke, Tedder, Cunningham, Alexander, Marshall, Eisenhower, Montgomery* (IWM)

release positions as shown on Map 2, in the seven various sectors, about 7 miles offshore. The somewhat impersonal code names of the seven sectors, JOSS, DIME, CENT, BARK West, BARK South, BARK East, ACID South, and ACID North, and the numbered landing beaches, give little impression of the sort of beach that was to be approached. In the event, models and pictures of the beaches were prepared and the landing troops were made familiar with the views during their training period without knowing, until they were proceeding on the last leg of their sea passage, where their destination lay. Not only was the view of the beach required, but also information about soundings, rocks, state of bottom, slope, and nature of beach.

More than 300 miles of coastline had to be examined before the invasion, and the survey indicated that there were not many beaches that combined an ideal approach from the sea and convenient access to roads ashore. Some thirty-two were declared possible, and in the event twenty-six were used. Much of the detailed reconnaissance of the beaches was performed by officers and men from submarines working inshore with chariots (a slow torpedo type weapon operated by two divers sitting astride) and collapsible canoes (folbots) fitted with infra-red gear. They made surveys that indicated slope of beach, nature of bottom, and general hazards. The task of the seven submarines shown in Map 2 was to mark the release positions of their respective convoys and to lay navigational aids in position to assist landing-craft flotillas in finding their beaches. One vital and useful development by the charioteers was the mobile diving unit, which was able to answer and meet the frequent demands for help when landing vehicles fouled their propellers.

Obviously there would be unseen snags, not the least being local currents caused by wind, and to a lesser extent tidal effects. A straightforward pattern, however, for the first batches ashore would be that the landing craft, usually LCA, would be marshalled in flotillas and directed by motor launches. The MLs would guide the flotillas as far as sonic buoys, which had been moored about 2 miles off each beach 24 hours earlier by the beacon submarines. The buoys were set to surface and to begin sounding signals early on 10 July. From the sonic buoy the final run-in would take place. Folbots with dim light directed seaward would supplement the sonic buoys where necessary.

The year 1943 was a significant one for the design and production of beach recovery equipment and of improved types of landing craft, of which those listed below are probably the best remembered. They played a prominent part in the Sicily landings. Such production is the more remarkable when it is recalled that little effective thought had been given to the subject before the outbreak of war in 1939, when there were many who declared that there was little likelihood of amphibious landings in the future. However, there were experts working in Combined Operations who argued the necessity for fast ships that could approach a shore under cover of darkness, carrying craft that could be used to put vehicles, reserves, and stores directly across beaches. Successful newcomers appear to have been ships and craft that could put tanks ashore. But one of the most effectual innovations was the newly developed amphibious DUKW, which could proceed through the water at $5\frac{1}{2}$ knots and then carry a load of $2\frac{1}{2}$ tons at high speed on land. Waterproofing of vehicles, tanks, and guns made great strides and enabled the effectual development of independent close fire support for newly landed troops. A further important development was the portable pontoon, which could quickly be assembled from rectangular tanks. Another highly successful latecomer was the rocket projector, which could produce an intensely shattering effect in more ways than one. The subject of landing craft and assault ships is well covered in Bernard Fergusson's *The Watery Maze*.

Here is a list of types of landing craft, with speeds roughly 8–10 knots:

LCA	landing craft assault (35 men)
LCF	landing craft flak, for anti-aircraft (500 tons)
LCG	landing craft gun, carrying two 4.7in guns (500 tons)
LCI	landing craft infantry, carrying 200 men (250 tons)
LCM	landing craft mechanised (30 tons)
LCP	landing craft personnel (9 tons)
LCS	landing craft support
LCT	landing craft tank (300 to 350 tons)
LCT(R)	landing craft tank rocket (500 tons)

Here is a list of types of landing ship, considerably larger than landing craft of course, and with speeds of 8 knots and above:

LSI(L)	landing ship infantry (large) to carry LCA
LSI(M)	landing ship infantry (medium)
LSI(S)	landing ship infantry (small)

LST   landing ship tank (2,000 tons)
LSH   headquarters ship with special communications

The LST and LCT were specially designed to disembark their tanks by ramp or other means direct on to the beach, but experience proved that this was not always practicable, as will be seen in Chapter 7, Western Assault.

A word by R. F. Stay about the newly developed rocket craft is of interest in view of the difficulties that were met. My thanks are also due to Rear-Adm T. W. Best and Cdr H. H. H. Mulleneux for information on this subject. Stay writes:

During the Sicily invasion I was serving as an eighteen-year-old ordinary seaman aboard a then unique type of landing craft, an LCT(R) or rocket ship. These were converted tank landing craft with the tank hold decked over and mounted with 1,000 5in fixed angle rocket projectors. These were fired by an electrical circuit from a contact at the base of the rocket. They were mostly HE, but we carried also two banks of ranging rockets filled with smoke or incendiary.

The method of use was for the rocket ships to form up line abreast behind the initial assault troops and lay down a creeping barrage firing over the top of the LCAs. The theory was that such was the intensity of the barrage that any defences would be demoralised. Having witnessed firing of a sister ship I can well believe it! The positioning of the ship was obtained by means of radar.

During firing no one was on the upper deck except the CO in an asbestos box on the bridge, conning the ship via a quartz glass window in the box. The first lieutenant was on the firing panel in the wheel-house immediately below the bridge, and the crew, apart from engine room ratings, were below the rocket deck. The deck was continuously sprayed with water for cooling, but none the less the ship had to be largely repainted after each firing.

The gun ships carried two 4.7s and the flak ships a mixture of pom-poms and Oerlikon cannon, and were manned by marines.

Experience in the Allied landings on the coast of north-west

Africa in November 1942 had shown the necessity for loading the landing ships in reverse of the way in which the ship would be unloaded. This was called strategic loading. The most immediately required equipment would therefore be the last to be embarked, and in Operation HUSKY this was to be the policy. Even so, matters can go wrong. Captain Frankcom, who was Assistant SNOL (Senior Naval Officer Landing) in the BARK West sector, where 1 Canadian Division was to be landed, comments on one aspect of strategic loading:

> There was a sudden SOS from the army, a day or two after the assault, for boots to be unloaded. The Canadian infantry had advanced so fast after the retreating Italians that their Canadian boots had worn out! As ships had been strategically loaded with ammunition on top, it wasn't easy to reach the boots!

Frankcom also describes the strenuous job facing an ASNOL in the July heat, and the task of coordinating and expediting the discharge of thirty odd ships in the anchorage. This meant climbing scrambling nets to ascertain in each ship the rate of discharge. Frankcom writes: 'Lord Louis Mountbatten arrived for a visit on D-day. A few hundred Italian prisoners were on the beach and became willing helpers with the handling of stores.'

But we are running ahead of schedule. It all sounds peaceful on this beach where many of the Italians showed little wish to fight, and either surrendered or fled to the north. There was still plenty of time for a strong and coordinated Axis defence to develop.

5 Naval Aspect

The task of the naval command was to ensure the timely and safe arrival of the assault forces at their beaches and to provide cover during disembarkation. But obviously the job did not end there. Fire support and maintenance would have to continue as long as the operation lasted. In general, bombardment by warships would not take place before touchdown, but thereafter would be on call.

Cunningham proposed to give effect to his intentions in the following manner:

1 To avoid as long as possible concentrating ships in the central Mediterranean and thus to avoid revealing the direction of attack.

2 Movements of convoys would conform to normal practice, with division into slow and fast groups. They would round Cape Bon in daylight in good time to arrive at the various rendezvous, and be provided with anti-aircraft support and warship escort.

3 There would be a covering force of battleships and aircraft carriers, concentrated in the Ionian Sea on the day before D-day to protect the eastern flank of the assault from possible interference by the Italian fleet. On D-day this force would be directed as if to threaten the west coast of Greece.

4 A cruiser force, supported if necessary by battleships, would cover the passage of the convoys along the North African coast.

5 At night the northern flank of the assaults was to be covered by cruisers and coastal forces, and the western flank by coastal forces only.

6 Adequate escort to be provided for follow-up and return convoys.

7 Naval forces would demonstrate to the westward of Sicily to contain the enemy's reserves.

8 Naval forces would continue to support and maintain the armies to the full extent of their requirements.

The Allied naval plan for HUSKY, issued by Cunningham on 20 May, indicated a very large and complicated operation: some 3,000 ships and major landing craft.

The main covering force (Force H), under Vice-Admiral Sir Algernon Willis, comprised the British battleships *Nelson*, *Rodney*, *Warspite*, and *Valiant* and the British aircraft carriers *Formidable* and *Indomitable*. In addition there was Force K, comprising the British cruisers *Newfoundland*, *Orion*, *Mauritius*, and *Uganda* of the 15th Cruiser Squadron (Rear-Admiral Harcourt) and six destroyers of 19th and 6th Destroyer Flotillas. These were assigned to the Eastern Task Force and allocated particular duties of convoy escort and, after arrival at the specified sector, bombardment of shore targets as called for, in much the same way as the American cruisers allocated to the Western Task Force.

Force H was to rendezvous at 6.00am, 9 July, the day before D-day, some 240 miles south-east of Malta (see Map 3). Then it would operate in the Ionian Sea to cover the eastern flank of the assault, following which it was to mislead the enemy high command by approaching the west coast of Greece. Two battleships, the *Howe* and the *King George V*, comprising Force Z, were to remain in the western basin as cover for the eastbound convoys, and in addition were to make a demonstration west of Sicily with the object of containing enemy reserves. These capital ships constituted a powerful fleet by any standards, and required an appropriate number of screening destroyers

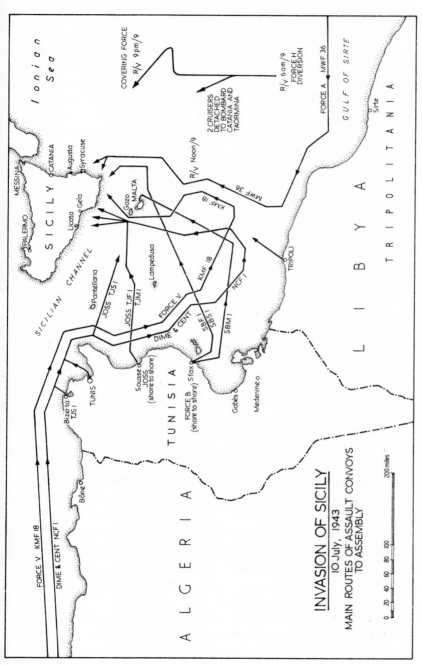

Map 3   Invasion of Sicily: main routes of assault convoys to assembly

in view of the known presence in the Mediterranean of eighteen U-boats and forty-five Italian submarines. Also to be allocated as required in support of Force H for special demonstrations was Force Q, the famous 12th Cruiser Squadron, consisting of the cruisers *Aurora* (broad pennant of CS12, Commodore Agnew), *Penelope, Cleopatra, Euryalus, Sirius,* and *Dido* – ships that had already seen rugged and prolonged service in the Mediterranean during the years 1941–2.

In order to execute the Sicily landings on the two stretches of the south and south-east coasts, 66,000 Americans had to be transported, some from America, some from North Africa, and 115,000 British soldiers from the Middle East, Tunisia, and Britain for the initial assaults. Follow-up troops would be required as the operation developed.

The American Western Naval Task Force was to come under the command of Vice-Admiral H. Kent Hewitt (flagship *Monrovia*), charged with the timely and accurate landing of General Patton's army at H-hour on D-day. This was to be divided as we have seen into three attack forces:

1 JOSS force, under Rear-Adm Conolly (flagship *Biscayne*), transporting 3 US Infantry Division under Major-Gen Truscott, escorted by the US cruisers *Brooklyn* and *Birmingham* and eight destroyers. See Maps 2 and 3 for routes of JOSS, DIME, and CENT forces.
2 DIME force, under Rear-Adm Hall (flag in *Samuel Chase*), transporting 1 US Infantry Division under Major-Gen Allen, escorted by the US cruisers *Savannah* and *Boise* and thirteen destroyers.
3 CENT force, under Rear-Adm Kirk (flag in *Ancon*), transporting 45 US Infantry Division under Major-Gen Middleton, escorted by the US cruiser *Philadelphia* and fifteen destroyers.

The British Eastern Naval Task Force was to come under the command of Admiral Sir Bertram Ramsay, flying his flag in the headquarters ship HMS *Antwerp*, charged with the timely and accurate landing of Montgomery's Eighth Army. This was divided into three attack forces:

1 Force A for ACID North and ACID South under Rear-Adm Troubridge, transporting the 5 and 50 British Divisions ship to shore, and also a tank battalion, an armoured regiment, and three commandos. Troubridge (NCF'A') was to fly his flag in the headquarters ship HMS *Bulolo*. See route of Forces A, B, and V in Maps 2 and 3. Part of Force A, earmarked to part company with the main body and steer westward in latitude 36°45′North, was bound for BARK East under the command of Captain Lord Ashbourne, SNOL at BARK East. Ashbourne, embarked in the headquarters ship *Keren*, was responsible for transporting 231 Brigade in a ship to shore passage, from Malta to BARK East near Marzamemi.

2 Force B for BARK South under Rear-Adm McGrigor (NCF'B'), transporting 51 Highland Division to Portopalo, shore to shore, and flying his flag in the headquarters ship HMS *Largs*.

3 Force V for BARK West under Read-Adm Vian (NCF'V'), flying his flag in the headquarters ship HMS *Hilary*, transporting 1 Canadian Division, ship to shore, south-west of Pachino, plus an armoured regiment, from the United Kingdom.

We have mentioned by name some of the bigger ships (cruisers and above), many of them well known, which were to take on specific tasks. It is obviously not practicable to name all the ships, but in order to appreciate the problems that faced the naval planners, it is interesting to take a close look at the following list of the types of ship that played a part in the Allied cause.

Types of Ship in Operation HUSKY

Type	British	American
Battleships	6	—
Aircraft carriers	2	—
Cruisers	10	5
Anti-aircraft	4	—
Fighter direction	2	—
Monitors	3	—
Gunboats	3	—
Minelayers	1	3
HQ ships	5	4
Destroyers	71	48
Escort vessels	35	—
Minesweepers	34	8
Major landing craft	319	190
Minor landing craft	715	510
Coastal craft	160	83
Submarines	23	—
Miscellaneous	58	28
LSIs manned by RN	8	—
Merchant and troop transports	155	66
Totals	1,614	945

There were also thirty-one Belgian, Dutch, Greek, Norwegian, and Polish ships, bringing the initial grand total to 2,590 vessels, later swelling to over 3,000. It should not escape notice that the two aircraft carriers had Fleet Air Arm squadrons comprising 100 aircraft, a priceless weapon of great mobility and flexibility with which to supplement the Allied air strength. For the next big amphibious operation after HUSKY the number of carriers was to be increased to five. The following were the squadrons present in the carriers during HUSKY:

Squadron No	HMS Indomitable	Squadron No	HMS Formidable
807	12 Seafire	885	5 Seafire
880	14 Seafire	888	14 Martlet
899	14 Seafire	893	14 Martlet
817	15 Albacore	820	12 Albacore

The first batch of troops and stores for assembly at North African ports sailed from America as early as 28 May 1943. From those ships, and others assembling at Oran and Algiers, were formed six of the assault and follow-up convoys destined for the CENT and DIME sectors of the Western assault. The convoy designation was NCF for the fast convoys, and NCS for the slow. To give an example of the timetable, NCS 1 left Oran on 4 July, steaming at 8 knots, and NCF 1 left Algiers on 6 July at 13 knots; the latter comprised the main assault convoy of Hewitt's Western Task Force carrying Patton's Seventh Army and assault craft and supplies for Sicily. There were, in particular, the control force flagship *Monrovia* (an HQ ship), seven store ships, and twenty-two combat loaders (LSI). Fast convoy NCF 2 was to sail from Algiers three days later, carrying a reserve of four troop transports, and to be joined by fast convoy KMF 19 (see below). NCF 1 and NCF 2 were to be followed by the slow follow-up convoys NCS 2, NCS 3, and NCS 4.

Convoys TJF 1 and TJS 1, $12\frac{1}{2}$ knots and $6\frac{1}{2}$ knots respectively, were to leave Tunisia bound for JOSS sector, the former on 5 July from Bizerta with 106 LCIs, and leaving Sousse 9 July; the latter leaving Tunis with 116 LCTs on 8 July. The routes shown on Map 3 do not necessarily give exact tracks but present some idea of the complexity of the plans to be prepared and issued.

KMF and KMS were the designations for the fast and slow convoys from the Clyde (K representing UK), bound for the Mediterranean, carrying 1 Canadian Division. They comprised the four assault and follow-up convoys for BARK West. They were enumerated KMF 18 and 19, and KMS 18 and 19, and their approximate routes may be seen on Map 3. Also on the map can be seen the route for the MW fast and slow convoys MWF 36 and MWS 36 in their long passage westward from the Middle East. The slow convoy MWS 36 was to leave Alexandria on 3 July at 8 knots, bound for sectors ACID North, ACID South, and BARK East, with thirty motor-transport store ships, fifteen LSTs, and two LSGs. They were to be joined off Malta by fifteen LSTs and forty-eight LCTs from Tripoli, and also by three oilers. The fast convoy MWF 36, which was to leave Port Said at 12 knots, 5 July, was to consist of one HQ ship and seventeen LSIs, also bound for sectors ACID North and South, and BARK East, with XIII Corps and XXX Corps of the Eighth Army. They would be joined by four LCIs from Tripoli.

The only losses among Allied convoys before their ships reached the assault area were suffered by convoy KMS 18 B, which lost the *City of Venice* and the *Saint Essylt* on 4 July, and the *Devis* on 5 July, all three off the North African coast; and by convoy MWS 36, which lost the *Shahjehan* on 6 July off Derna. U-boats were responsible in each case. That there were no bigger losses is a tribute to the continuous day and night cover provided in the Mediterranean both in the air and by supporting ships.

Perhaps the most direct and shortest journeys were those taken by the SB convoys leaving Sfax on 7 July and 8 July for the rendezvous off Malta on the afternoon of 9 July. Their ultimate destination was the BARK South sector, and they carried 51 Division. SBS 1 steamed at 6 knots and comprised one LST and twenty-nine LCTs. SBM 1 proceeded at 8 knots and included twenty-six LSTs. SBF 1 sped along at 13 knots and had, in addition to McGrigor's HQ ship *Largs*, four LSIs. They were to pick up six LCIs off Malta before proceeding on the last lap of 50 miles for BARK South.

It is not practicable to give particulars of all the assault and follow-up convoys, nor would they be of general interest. But extracts from individual descriptions will be included later, so as to record the impressions and views of just a few of the many thousands of troops proceeding towards their particular beaches.

It should be realised that with the various divisions and sub-divisions carried in the American and British convoys there would be an appropriate proportion of specialist troops concerned with artillery, engineering, transport, signals, airfield construction, medicine, surgery, and supply and administration generally. American shore units incidentally had a much higher proportion of men with technical training than the British. Supporting and covering forces for the Western Naval Task Force were divided between the three attack force commanders, and included five US cruisers and the British Monitor *Abercrombie*.

The amazing fact is that until ships and convoys put to sea for the final lap their destination was kept a closely guarded secret to be revealed by a senior officer at the right moment. All, by this time, were closely familiar with the pictures and models of the particular beach on which they were to land. But, *where* the beach was remained known only to the few.

The following extract comes from a letter written to the author by Vice-Admiral Lord Ashbourne and remarks on the question of secrecy:

I was there myself in the form of a Senior Naval Officer Landing (SNOL), with captain's rank, wearing four stripes and responsible for putting 231 Brigade ashore at Marzamemi in Sector BARK East, 5 miles north of Cape Passero. We did our planning at Cairo, and our rehearsals in the Gulf of Suez and Aqaba. Four of us SNOLs flew out to Cairo in April 1943. Before that we were planning at Norfolk House in London. I gave my brother (a wartime colonel) lunch at the Senior one day. After lunch we both excused ourselves as we had to return to our respective offices. We both walked down Pall Mall together, turned into St James's Square together, and entered Norfolk House together. Until then neither of us knew the other was in the Sicily business.

This speaks well for the security of HUSKY. After referring to the tedious and sticky business of planning and rehearsals at Cairo in midsummer, he writes:

We came north through the canal 3 days ahead of schedule, to fox the Italians. While waiting the 3 days at Port Said, the soldiers got restive and clamoured for a run ashore. I saw them march through Port Said and they were a most impressive sight. I remember thinking that if the Italians could have seen them they would have packed up fighting altogether and called it a day.

Weather was rough the evening before the landing. We had been told during the planning stage that the army must be put ashore regardless of cost. I therefore signalled to my LSIs (*Strathnaver*, *Otranto*, and *Keren* – I was in *Keren*) telling them, in the event of the weather continuing foul, where they were to run themselves aground to ensure getting their soldiers landed.

As it got light I remember getting a thrill at seeing the coastline looking exactly as the army and RAF had told us – the army having made wonderful models, and the RAF having taken splendid photographs.

The troops seem to have placed great faith in what the navy could do. This attitude is noticeable in many letters describing the operation, and is remarked upon by Cunningham in a letter to the First Sea Lord in which he expresses concern at the prospect of having to turn back 3,000 ships at short notice should the weather turn foul. 'The soldiers seem to think,' he wrote, 'that they will be landed at the exact spot, the weather will be perfect, and that naval gunfire will silence all opposition.'

There were many problems quite apart from the timing and routeing of the convoys, and consideration had to be given not only to weather, sea, swell, and surf possibilities, but to such matters as minefields, fuelling of escorts, the comprehension of naval communications in merchant ships, and the best tactical manoeuvres to be adopted by the ships of the convoy at times of submarine or aircraft attack. More particularly considerable experience and training were required for the handling of landing craft and for efficient disembarkation of the big landing ships, with all the necessary equipment, weapons, rations, and water.

Although the Allies were now in total occupation of Tunisia, and operating to the full such ports as Bizerta, Tunis, Sousse, and Sfax, it was felt that the control of the narrows between Cape Bon and Sicily could easily be affected by the continued Axis possession of the island of Pantelleria. The island lies 40 miles from the Tunisian coast and 60 miles from the Sicilian coast, and had been developed by Mussolini in 1937 as a counter to Malta. By 1943 it had strong fixed defences and was garrisoned by 12,000 men. But what was more important was its possession of an airfield that the Allies considered essential for their use in order to supplement the fighters operating from Malta.

Earlier in the war, at the end of 1940, Admiral Keyes, who was then Director of Combined Operations, had proposed that Pantelleria should be captured. This project was carefully considered by the chiefs of staff in spite of opposition from Cunningham, who at that time considered it a 'wild-cat scheme' when compared with other essentials. The scheme was dropped. But from the middle of May 1943 the Mediterranean was once again open for ships, and Cunningham felt that because of its strategic position Pantelleria should be captured. Eisenhower agreed. Preliminary bombing and bombardment began the softening process, and an assault force was prepared under the command of Rear-Admiral McGrigor. This force sailed from Sfax and Sousse on 10 June. Heavy bombardment by sea and air was followed by a summons to surrender, and a landing of the assault force, which achieved that end. The surrender of the smaller island of Lampedusa, 80 miles to the south of Pantelleria, followed on 12 June.

Meanwhile the great stream of landing craft and landing ships built in America had been proceeding eastward across the Atlantic to such assembly ports as Oran, Algiers, Bizerta, Sfax, and Suez. LSTs would be carrying LCTs, tanks, guns, and vehicles, where practicable; LCIs would proceed in company. The landing craft were in many cases crewed by reservist officers and men from British warships being repaired in American yards. They took quickly to their responsible and somewhat hazardous tasks.

Vice-Adm Kent Hewitt, USN, commander Western assault
(USN)

It is interesting to hear of the crowded conditions in many ships. Admiral Hewitt's flagship in the Western Naval Task Force, the *Monrovia*, which accompanied DIME force, is a case in point. Embarked were the Admiral and his staff, together with a fighter control group of the Army Air Force, and General Patton, commanding the Seventh Army, with his staff. Three separate code rooms had to be provided, and *Monrovia* had to accommodate 126 officers and 670 men over and above her normal complement of 48 officers and 566 men.

During June rehearsals of embarkation and disembarkation took place, together with various exercises, and by the end of the month, the loading of the assault and follow-up convoys had been completed. Admiral Ramsay and his staff were transferred from Cairo to Malta, whither Cunningham had already shifted his headquarters. The old Admiralty House in Valetta had been restored to use, as had the Commander-in-Chief's bastion at Lascaris, with its wonderful view of the Grand Harbour, now filling with ships and landing craft.

On 3 July Cunningham sailed from Algiers for Malta in the cruiser *Uganda*. He writes of his feelings as the day drew nearer for the great launching, and of his concern at the great responsibility for landing 160,000 troops and all their varied impedimenta; he thought of the possible confusion that might be caused by just an error in a solitary figure. The day for the first Allied invasion of enemy territory was near. Eisenhower and Alexander arrived in Malta on 8 July, and were accommodated by the Governor. Eisenhower was provided with office accommodation alongside Cunningham in the Lascaris bastion. This was reminiscent of their shared headquarters in the tunnel at Gibraltar, which they had used before the successful TORCH landings in North Africa just 8 months earlier. It seemed a good omen.

To end this chapter, which describes the naval plan, it is appropriate to recall the inspiring message sent by the naval commander of the operation, Admiral of the Fleet Sir Andrew Cunningham, to all ships on the eve of the operation:

   (i) We are about to embark on the most momentous enterprise of the war – striking for the first time at the enemy
in his own land.

 (ii) Success means the opening of the 'Second Front' with all
that implies, and the first move towards the rapid and
decisive defeat of our enemies.

(iii) Our object is clear and our primary duty is to place this
vast expedition ashore in the minimum time and subse-
quently to maintain our military and air forces as they
drive relentlessly forward into enemy territory.

(iv) In the light of this duty, great risks must be and are to be
accepted. The safety of our ships and all distracting considerations are to be relegated to second place, or dis-
regarded as the accomplishment of our primary duty may
require.

 (v) On every commanding officer, officer, and rating rests the
individual and personal duty of ensuring that no flinching
in determination or failure of effort on his own part will
hamper this great enterprise.

(vi) I rest confident in the resolution, skill, and endurance of
you all to whom this momentous enterprise is entrusted.

This great sailor, likened by many to Nelson, left no doubt
in the minds of all as to what was expected of them.

6 Air Aspect

Of the intense dedication to duty and gallant individual service performed by members of the Allied air forces there can be no question, yet for one reason and another those forces cannot, in retrospect, be given the praise one would have hoped to give. It is not possible to lay the blame specifically here or there, mainly because the principal factor was lack of coordination in a command structure that was most complex. At the top of the Mediterranean air command was Air Chief Marshal Sir Arthur Tedder, with at least sixteen commands under his direction, of which it is sufficient here, in considering HUSKY, to mention only the more senior posts.

The prime policy was the destruction of enemy air power, and this strategic task was allocated by the senior American air officer under Tedder, Lt-Gen Carl Spaatz, commanding the North-west African Air Force (NAAF), to Major-Gen James Doolittle's North-west African Strategic Air Force (NASAF), consisting of seventy-three squadrons. But Spaatz had also under his command the North-west African Tactical Air Force (NATAF), consisting of forty-three squadrons under Air Marshal Arthur Coningham, which included the XII US Air Support Command (US XII ASC), under Colonel Hickey, USAAF, charged with direct air support for the Western Task Force during the forthcoming amphibious operation. Also within the NAAF under Spaatz was the North-west African Coastal Air Force (NACAF), consisting of thirty squadrons under the command of Air Marshal Sir Hugh Lloyd. There was also the Malta Air Command, with twenty-six squadrons, charged with fighter protection for assault forces within 50 miles of the island. That command was held by Air Vice-Marshal Sir Keith Park, but was under the general control of NATAF. In support of the Eastern Task Force was the Western Desert Air Force (WDAF) under Air Vice-Marshal Harry Broadhurst, operating from the Tripoli area until such time as bases could be established in Sicily. Farther east was the Middle East Air Command (MEAC), under Air Chief Marshal Sir William Sholto Douglas, consisting of seventeen squadrons, with a coastal force of sixteen squadrons (the No 201 Naval Cooperation Group RAF) under Air Vice-Marshal T. A. Langford-Sainsbury for convoy protection, and an Air Defence Force (for fighter protection) with eighteen squadrons under Air Vice-Marshal R. E. Saul.

The US Naval Historian, Rear-Adm S. E. Morison, has, in view of criticism of lack of tactical fighter support, discussed the problem in his *US Naval Operations in World War II*, Vol IX, p 22. Referring to NAAF, he writes:

> Although this command included over 400 planes, it would give no advance assurance to Army or Navy as to the kind and quality of the support they could expect on D-day or thereafter. This refusal stemmed from the reluctance of top air commanders to sacrifice flexibility: 'Tactical' might be wanted to support 'Strategic' in action against enemy air forces.

Recalling the effective support given by escort carriers off Casablanca in the TORCH operation, General Patton begged Admiral Hewitt to procure some, remarking, 'You can get your Navy planes to do anything you want, but we can't get the Air Force to do a goddam thing.' In fact there was at that moment a vital call for escort carriers for anti-submarine work in the Atlantic. They could not be spared for the HUSKY landings over and above the two big fleet carriers *Indomitable* and *Formidable*, whose main task was to support and cover the battleships.

The argument in favour of the tactical use as against the

strategic use of aircraft is obviously one that can only be decided by consideration of all the prevailing factors. There was nobody other than Tedder with a long experience of probable requirements. His policy was flexibility, and it was for this reason that all air forces in the Mediterranean area were under his control. They included all the NAAF, as described above, and therefore covered coastal, strategic, and tactical requirements. The greatest fault in the organisation was the wide dispersal of individual headquarters, caused largely by the fact that, despite the need for HUSKY planning, the war in Tunisia did not end until May.

There were to be three main phases in the air plan. The first was to begin as soon as the enemy had been defeated in Tunisia, and was to comprise systematic bombing of Italian industry and Axis airfields, care being taken to distribute the attacks so as to give no hint of where the amphibious invasion would be. RAF bombers from the UK were to attack Italy and Germany, while bombers from the Middle East were to attack the Dodecanese and Aegean islands. Until 3 July, a week before D-day, strategic bombing attacks were to be made against principal enemy airfields in Sardinia, Sicily, and southern Italy.

The second phase for a whole week before D-day was to aim at destroying enemy fighters and communications in Sicily and Sardinia. In order to maintain surprise, however, beach defences were not to be attacked.

The third phase was to be the all-out attack on local airfields coordinated with the attacks to be made by land forces. It was considered that the day after D-day would be the most hazardous for ships approaching or lying off the beaches, since by that time the main Allied concentration points would have been revealed. The fighters would then be needed to transfer from their offensive roles to the task of protecting approaching ships from enemy bombers. Herein lay the advantage of Tedder's policy of flexibility. In general the North-west African Coastal Air Force would have the duty of protecting ships from North

African ports, whereas the No 201 Naval Co-operation Group RAF would be responsible for ships from the Middle East. The ships lying off the landing beaches could expect day and night fighter protection from airfields in Malta and Pantelleria until nearby Sicilian airfields were captured. The regime of fighter direction ships was relatively new, having begun in a modest way in the *Formidable* in 1941. Until fighter control could be established ashore, it was intended that this duty should be undertaken in the headquarters ships.

With reference to the readiness of strategic aircraft answering tactical calls, Morison records that the North-west African Coastal Air Force cooperated to the limit of its capacity. ' "Coastal",' he says, 'was predominantly British, just as "tactical" was predominantly American.' Capacity to help depended upon availability of serviceable aircraft, airfields, personnel, and the degree of urgency of a particular task – a very subjective factor. It is presumed that no military force would give anything less than the limit of its capacity. What is commendable is the relatively small number of ships lost from air attack, during the presence of so many on passage and while lying off Sicily or in harbour.

No attempt will be made here to delineate the exact duties of the various commands and sub-commands and their relations. It may be helpful, however, to record the various forces responsible for air protection of, say, a large convoy proceeding eastward from Gibraltar to Alexandria.

The first responsible authority would be Air Headquarters Gibraltar, a relic of the arrangement agreed for TORCH; previously this had been under Coastal Command. Protection by Gibraltar would end as the convoy passed the meridian of Cape Tenez in Algeria, and be taken over by the North-west African Coastal Air Force under Air Vice-Marshal Lloyd, who was responsible to Spaatz for the defence of shipping and also for fighter protection of ports and airfields in the western and central Mediterranean areas. Excluded from NACAF control, however, were the waters within 50 miles of Malta, wherein fighter protection was to be provided by Malta Air Command under Air Vice-Marshal Park.

East of Tripoli as far as the Levant coast, and outside a distance of 40 miles from the North African coast, protection of shipping was assured by No 201 Naval Co-operation Group, RAF, under Air Vice-Marshal Langford-Sainsbury. This group had been set up in December 1941 following repeated demands from Cunningham for aircraft and airmen that would meet specifically naval requirements, especially in identification and reconnaissance. This was in the grim days when, as C-in-C Mediterranean, he suffered the loss of so many ships, primarily through great strength of the Axis air forces, but also through lack of dependable reports as to enemy movements. By early 1942 he was commenting on the 'strikingly efficient and valuable' work carried out by this group.

Protection for ships closer than 40 miles from the North African coast was available from the Air Defences Eastern Mediterranean Command, which was also responsible for providing fighter protection of ports and airfields in the eastern Mediterranean.

In a smaller but very active way the Fleet Air Arm provided aircraft for anti-shipping and anti-submarine duties, to the extent of six squadrons dispersed among the above air commands except Air Defences Eastern Mediterranean, which was controlled ultimately by the Middle East Air Commander, Air Chief Marshal Sir William Sholto Douglas, in Cairo.

How different now was the air situation from that of a year before, when Axis possession of the airfields that dominated the narrows between Sicily and Tunisia and between Crete and Cyrenaica, had practically isolated Malta and had brought that island to the verge of collapse. Now in July 1943, excluding transports, the total number of aircraft available to the Allies was in round figures 3,500, of which 2,500 were serviceable. In Malta maintenance, service, repair facilities, communications, and airport space had all improved; and these facilities would be set up in Sicily at the earliest opportunity.

The Axis totals no longer matched those of the Allies, their figures, excluding transports, being of the order of 1,750. Moreover, although the Germans had strengthened their air forces generally in the Mediterranean since May 1943, they were widely dispersed, the Greece and Crete areas benefiting at the expense of the areas round Sicily.

In spite of the Allied numerical superiority in aircraft, and because of Tedder's insistence on flexibility, there was no specific air allocation to either the Eastern or Western Task Forces, and this became the subject of criticism by Admiral Kirk, who commanded the CENT sector of the Western Naval Task Force. Through lack of coordination and difficulties in identification, friendly planes were often shot down by friendly troops, whereas enemy aircraft were allowed to come in and play havoc. Admiral Kirk reported:

> No control over fighter patrol was delegated to the CENT Attack Force. No bombers were on call. No fighter protection to spotting planes was provided. At no time was the Force informed concerning the degree of air control exercised by our forces and as to what enemy attack might be expected. The air battle was separate and foreign, apparently unconcerned about the situation in the CENT area.

These were very strong words, but such comment is justifiable if lessons are to be learned and future planning to be more considerate of the tactical side of the problem. The above remarks should be considered in the light of those of another author, Roskill, in *War at Sea*, Vol III, part I, p 140. He considers that the matter should be viewed through a wider lens than could possibly be available to an individual assault commander. 'Though the Air Plan suffered through lack of co-ordination with those of the other services,' he writes, 'the accomplishments of the Air Forces – many of which could not possibly be seen from the assault beaches – none the less remain impressive.' He emphasises the comparative immunity of ships from air attacks during approach and assault, and the big part played by the air commands. Cunningham, who had fought through the Mediterranean campaign for almost four years, with only a short break, said in his despatch that it appeared almost magical that great fleets of ships could remain anchored on the enemy's coast, within 40 miles of the main aerodromes, with only such slight losses as were incurred.

A great deal of thought was given during the planning stage to the use of airborne troops, and in the early stages it was proposed that airborne divisions be dropped in the toe of Italy to obstruct Axis reinforcement of Sicily. In due course, however, Eisenhower and Alexander agreed that the essential role of airborne troops was the softening of beach defences during the assault phase, and that their most apt employment would be to work inland from the beaches to secure important features on the line of advance. While it was realised that naval gunfire could be brought to bear for the neutralisation of certain shore defences, it was thought that a greater degree of control would be possible with troops quickly transported by air. But this was to raise further problems when it was known that air transports and gliders could only be provided in limited numbers. In the event airborne troops were to suffer from quite a number of unforeseen or unavoidable mishaps, such as sudden weather change and erroneous identification.

A big feature of the air plan, though not much heard of, was surreptitious reconnaissance and systematic photography, undertaken with the object of gaining the fullest intelligence of existing conditions and the changes that were taking place in Sicily. The Italians were tired of the war and becoming increasingly reluctant to cooperate with the Germans. Mussolini, whose days were already numbered, was losing his hold, and there was a plot to overthrow him. It was Mussolini, nevertheless, who felt certain that Sicily would be the object of a forthcoming Allied invasion, whereas Hitler regarded Sardinia as the most likely place of attack. From the Axis point of view Sicily was only one of several areas that seemed to be threatened, and whose defences must somehow or other be strengthened. Psychological warfare was playing its part, as Churchill fully intended it should when referring vaguely to the unspecified soft underbelly; and Operation MINCE-MEAT, described earlier, intensified the uncertainty. It was up to the Italian Ambrosio and the German Kesselring to agree if they could as to which objective should take preference in the matter of defences.

Gone were the days when the Axis enjoyed numerical superiority at sea or in the air. There was little trust or co-operation between the Italians and the Germans. In the spring of 1943 Mussolini had at first refused a German offer of rein-forcements in Sicily; but by June he was ready to accept. Indeed by June he was begging for reinforcements, not only in the matter of troops and artillery but for 2,000 aircraft. The Germans for their part were now unable and unwilling to spare any reserves for Italian disposal, either in troops or equipment, and were beginning to prepare for an Italian collapse. For this they had secret plans for the transfer of German troops from Russia and France to take over military control in the event of Italy attempting to give up the war. At the time of the Allied invasion of Sicily the defence of the island was nominally in the hands of the Italian General Guzzoni and his Italian Sixth Army, backed up by two reduced, but still tough, German panzer divisions.

Despite the great strength of the combined Allied air forces, there were never enough aircraft and facilities to satisfy all the demands for air support, convoy protection, offensive opera-tions, patrols, and reconnaissance. Much of the work against enemy bases went on unseen or unrecorded. Fighter protection for the ships in a large convoy was always a problem, but the task could be helped by concentrating available fighters and placing them under the control of a fighter direction ship.

Despite extensive use of radar in ships, identification of friend or foe continued to remain an inexact factor. The forthcoming operation was to include airborne assaults, during which care had to be taken to look out for two groups of troop-

68

carrying aircraft approaching the south-west corner of Sicily after dark on 9 July, the evening before D-day. The first group (150 aircraft in the Eastern assault) would pass close to Malta and drop paratroops in the Syracuse area. The second (250 aircraft in the Western assault) would drop paratroops in the Gela area.

Anti-aircraft gunfire from ships and craft was subject to restrictive orders. Merchant ships and landing craft lying off beaches were to engage aircraft only after naval escort vessels had opened fire. But naval ships and merchant ships would in all circumstances be free to open fire on multi-engined aircraft not recognised as friendly. Single-engined aircraft would be engaged only if recognised as hostile. Fire was not to be opened above 6,000ft when night fighters were operating over the convoys or beaches.

It all sounds so logical but it is questionable whether compliance was practicable in the heat of battle, as we shall hear from an observer, C. Collier, in ACID North sector:

> We approached our release position off Cape Negro in the US Liberty Ship *Colin P Kelly*, and anchored and commenced discharging according to requirements. Bombing attacks by enemy aircraft continued throughout the day and many aircraft of both sides were being shot down. From my recollections I feel sure the first wave of aircraft swept along the beaches and all bore British markings. They bombed before we realised it was so. After this all ships fired at everything.

Arrangements for air reconnaissance during the operation were based on the assumption that the principal Italian warships would remain in harbour, the *Littorio* battleships at Spezia, cruisers at Genoa, and Cavour class battleships at Taranto. These were the places to watch. An air torpedo force was to stand by ready to strike if reconnaissance should report that warships had put to sea. Heavy bombers were also available for this purpose. In addition photographic reconnaissance of enemy bases could be made twice daily. Anti-submarine patrols were flown daily on reconnaissance in both the western and eastern Mediterranean to hunt and immobilise submarines that might be found converging on the convoy routes. Air-sea rescue units were stationed in North Africa, Malta, and the Middle East.

A story is told by Admiral Vian in his *Action This Day* concerning a fortuitous move during the long journey of convoy KMF 18, which left the United Kingdom on 28 June bound for the BARK West sector in Sicily. Vian was flying his flag in HMS *Hilary* and had twelve personnel ships in company. With him in the headquarters ship were Mountbatten, the Chief of Combined Operations; General Simonds in command of 1 Canadian Division; and Brigadier Laycock – a tempting bait for any submarine. They arrived safely at and passed Gibraltar into the Mediterranean on 5 July. But on the following day, being well ahead of schedule, Vian made a reversal of course. As the signal was hoisted, the escorts of the anti-submarine screen swung round and sped away, so as to be in station when the turn was completed. The reversal of course, however, came as an unpleasant surprise to a U-boat which, unknown to the convoy, was hoping to attack after dark. Detected now by the screen, the U-boat was attacked by the British sloops *Whimbrel* and *Cygnet*. Depth charges drove the submarine to the surface, with her bows rising at a steep angle; there she remained for a minute or two before plunging stern first into the depths.

What reconnaissance might not be able to provide in the way of intelligence was more than compensated for at the time by information obtained by intercepting and breaking the enemy's ULTRA secrets, the story of which has been written by Group Captain F. Winterbotham. Referring to the ULTRA signals, General Alexander has said: 'The knowledge not only of the enemy's precise strength and disposition but also how, when, and where he intends to carry out his operation has brought a new dimension into the prosecution of the war.'

Winterbotham, who was the genius behind the breaking of

ULTRA, and who knew Kesselring before the war, writes:

> As you know, we had full details of the whereabouts and
> strengths of all the Axis forces in Sicily well before D day for
> HUSKY, but the Axis operation was in fact commanded by the
> Italians. Nevertheless we did get Kesselring's reports to Hitler
> on how the operation was going, with, at first, his optimistic
> reports of Montgomery being held at Catania.

By early July 1943 in Sicily there were in all about 200,000
Italian and 32,000 German troops in addition to 30,000
Luftwaffe groundsmen. This number was composed of Italian
defence forces practically around the whole coast, together
with four Italian divisions and two German panzer divisions.
One of the latter, the Hermann Goering Division, arrived
from the mainland only a few days before the Allies struck,
having been sent by Kesselring, who was one of the few who
refused to be taken in by the MINCEMEAT deception. The
German divisions were not up to strength in troops and armour,
but were experienced and well disciplined.

Briefly, the Axis troops in Sicily were deployed in three
categories. First were the men belonging to the coastal divisions
and coastal defences, thinly spread, though great in number,
round the lengthy perimeter of Sicily; they were mainly
Italian reservists. Second were the port defence groups,
manning what were regarded as strongpoints of defence
batteries and anti-aircraft guns, with special regard to the
strength of such ports as Palermo, Messina, and Catania. Third
were the six mobile divisions of the Italian and German armies,
which were to be kept in relatively central positions away from
the coast, ready for instant deployment, while the assaulting
forces were being held back by the coastal troops.

There was some difference of opinion between Guzzoni and
Kesselring as to the best disposition of the two German mobile
divisions, and a compromise was agreed whereby one should
stay in a good position to defend western Sicily and in particular Palermo, and the other be prepared for Allied landings

somewhere in the east or south-east. Guzzoni believed the Allies would land on a broad front, and that the main thrust lines would not be evident for some time.

In all it was a formidable Axis force, the Germans being particularly tough. The fortress areas and main fixed defences were of a fairly high standard, with emplaced guns and a fire control system. There were pillboxes and wire obstacles along certain stretches, and the existence of minefields was likely.

There seemed to be no shortage of intelligence groups within the assaulting forces. Colonel H. Quill, RM, writes:

> When D-day drew near I took with me Commander Rodd (interrogation), and Lieutenants Croxton and Solomon (intelligence and Italian), Lieutenant Bullen (security and Italian), Captain Lloyd (Army maps). With two jeeps we landed at Avola, later by-passed the Army, and reached Messina before anyone. We took up an excellent lookout post in Messina lighthouse and with a large captured telescope could observe enemy activities on the mainland.

One almost expects them to receive the surrender of the island, and it sounds at first like a taste of good things to come. But in fact right up to D-day, in spite of all the Allied bombing, the big train ferries were still operating across the Straits of Messina, and Axis reinforcements and supplies were pouring in from Italy.

It is recorded that one air photograph taken before D-day by an Intelligence Officer of the Highland Division revealed a party of women bathers at one of the assault beaches. The deduction in this case was that at least that particular beach would be free of mines and obstacles – and so it proved.

7 Western Assault

A signal from Admiral Cunningham on the morning of 4 July 1943 – 'Carry out Operation HUSKY' – gave the initial order for the operation to begin, and this was followed by his stirring message (already quoted), which called forth the 'individual and personal duty' of everyone concerned in this momentous expedition. The routeing and the timing of departure and arrival had been carefully worked out so that the various convoys would meet as required at the rendezvous, but, as luck would have it, the weather was to play a big part. On the morning of 9 July, the day before D-day, as various convoys from east and west were beginning to approach their appointed rendezvous near Malta, the weather began to deteriorate and it came on to blow hard from the north-west. The result was to raise a short choppy sea, especially along that part of the coast which was to be assaulted by the Americans. Craft moving in northwards to the beaches would be in danger of being swamped and foundering, and the carefully produced time-table might be seriously affected. It was already too late to amend the plans; a postponement of 24 hours might produce chaos, and a cancellation was unthinkable. Fortunately the deterioration was recognised by the meteorologists as an abrupt local change due to a mistral. The experts advised that moderation would probably follow that night.

Cunningham decided to let matters take their course, but his anxiety was scarcely relieved as he watched, during the afternoon, flotillas of landing craft proceeding to sea from Malta 'literally burying themselves with spray flying over them in solid sheets' as they plunged their way to the assault positions 60 miles away.

As forecast by the meteorologists, the wind began to moderate at 10.00pm, having risen during the day from 15 knots to 30 or 35. Later that evening Cunningham watched an airborne force of 134 gliders towed by Dakotas pass over Malta on their way to support the Eighth Army landings on the south-east coast. Regrettably, at least one-third of the gliders were released by their tugs too soon and, owing to excessive head winds and severe gusts, came down in the sea just short of their objective.

Meanwhile Admiral Hewitt's Western Force, having assembled 5 miles west of Malta at 6.00pm, proceeded northwards to find the release positions for the JOSS, DIME, and CENT sectors, marked respectively by the British submarines *Safari*, *Shakespeare*, and *Seraph*. Men in the LCTs and LCIs were drenched with the breaking seas, and seasickness was rife, but the force pressed on at the prescribed speed, intent on making the first landing at 2.45am 10 July. Morison states that at times the LCTs were slowed down to $2\frac{1}{2}$ knots and the LCIs were taking seas solid. There was much concern as to whether the force could keep to schedule. In the event, both JOSS and DIME forces were on time at the release points, but there had been moments when Hewitt had seriously considered making a signal to Cunningham advising postponement because of excessive wind and sea. A serious problem was the allowance to be made for drift and leeway caused by the beam wind.

Morison writes of the final approach in a night landing where everything ahead was uncertain. Ships and craft were shrouded in darkness but the shore was dimly visible. A few mistakes and the plan might be utterly wrecked. There could be no half measures. And what about surprise? Had that been achieved? It was clear that the enemy had not been completely surprised, though the strong wind and high sea had led many of the defendants to conclude, 'Tonight they cannot come'. Nevertheless one of the folbots from a beacon submarine had been seen from Gela beach, and five convoys steering north on the evening of 9 July had been spotted and reported by an Italian plane. At 1.00am, 10 July, Guzzoni declared a state of emergency, and only 6 hours earlier German forces in Sicily had been alerted. Was it perhaps too late? There was an air of relief about the foul weather among many of the Italian officers of the coastal divisions. Sicilians described their impressions to Morison the next morning with understandable exaggeration: 'There were thousands of vessels in the roadstead; one couldn't see the horizon for ships. Thousands of troops were landing every minute.'

Morison relates the story about an American news correspondent who was one of the first to land, and who spoke Italian well. He advanced quickly to a beach command post that had been abandoned by the Italians. The telephone rang. The news correspondent then found himself having a conversation with an Italian general. The general complained that he had been roused by a disturbing report about Americans landing in his sector. Surely this could not be true, especially on such a wild night. The news man reassured the general. All was well on the beaches. The parties then hung up, both well satisfied.

The enemy may not have been taken completely by surprise, but certainly he was not ready for what was now taking place. Guzzoni correctly deduced that there would not be any Allied landings to the west of Licata. He therefore ordered his mobile Axis forces in western Sicily to move eastward.

A glance at Map 2 will show that JOSS sector on the left was a little more sheltered from the north-west than DIME and CENT sectors to the right. JOSS forces, under Admiral Conolly in his flagship the *Biscayne*, closed correctly on the reference vessels and the submarine beacon, and all JOSS groups arrived at their correct transport areas and, except for the first few flights, were able to land at their respective beaches on time.

DIME sector and, to a greater extent, CENT sector had

Licata bombarded by US cruiser, 10 July 1943 (USN)

stronger winds and rougher seas than at JOSS. Although they were fairly punctual as 1st section and 2nd section respectively of convoy NCF 1 in the approach to Sicily, the two sections suffered some delays owing to unexpected alterations of course necessary to allow for the drift experienced by small craft. Although convoy speed was increased to compensate for this, LCTs and LCIs were unable to keep up and gradually fell astern. At one time DIME force consisted of a long single column of two cruisers and eleven transports flanked on one side by a column of LCTs and on the other side LCIs, the columns ever increasing in length. In spite of difficulties DIME force, under Admiral Hall, flying his flag in the transport *Samuel Chase*, reached its assigned area 40 minutes after midnight, and within 15 minutes was lowering landing craft.

76

Hewitt, in company in his flagship *Monrovia*, observed this with satisfaction, and later reported that the execution of the approach from the standpoint of navigation and seamanship was one of the highlights of the operation. CENT force under Kirk, flying his flag in the *Ancon*, reached the assigned area within 5 minutes of the arrival of DIME force. The submarines being no longer required for beacon duties withdrew under escort, too valuable to remain in these hazardous waters. An air raid over Gela had been reported earlier.

The shoreward movement of the waves of landing craft after their launching and assembly at the transport anchorages was guided by control vessels such as coastal craft, submarine chasers, and minesweepers. There was initially some light opposition, but the most disagreeable factor was the surf breaking on the beaches, causing a number of landing craft to broach to.

The landings in CENT sector were generally unopposed, probably because of a preliminary bombardment by destroyers, which had opened fire for 15 minutes before the first landing at 2.45am. The fire was lifted just before the first wave landed, but it was sufficiently effective to enable General Middleton's 45 US Division to land in the vicinity of Scoglitti and to establish a bridgehead earlier than planned. At two other beaches in the CENT sector heavy surf and extensive minefields caused considerable delay and confusion. Although at one time there was a mass of stranded craft and scattered shore parties, additional landing craft kept arriving from the transports and for some time added to the confusion and led to further losses and casualties.

Every large troop unit ashore included a shore fire control party, which could communicate by 'walkie-talkie' radio with the cruisers or destroyers that were in company providing fire support. In this matter the Americans were on the whole prepared to use naval gunfire in support more freely than the British, and in view of the greater opposition they met on this first day perhaps it was as well.

Horizon almost obscured by US landing craft, 10 July 1943
(USN)

The 1 US Division (under General Allen), landing in Admiral
Hall's DIME sector, were more fortunate than those of Kirk's
forces, so many of whom had been stranded in the CENT
sector. They encountered little resistance, though there were
casualties from mines and also from Italian fire in spite of good
naval fire support. However, Gela was captured by 8am and
1 US Division was soon working its way inland. Air attacks
on the shipping off Gela began at 4.30am, and in one of these
the destroyer *Maddox* of Kirk's force was sunk with heavy loss
of life. The absence of adequate fighters to protect the anchorage was deplored in a report of proceedings, and it was stated
that the enemy had almost complete control of the air over the
beachhead. It is only fair to add that as dawn broke on 9 July

the largest concentration of air power ever assembled in the Mediterranean began an offensive on enemy targets, and in particular on airfields to destroy bombers and fighters as well; by daylight, 10 July, Allied fighters were covering the beaches, but it was impracticable to cover all the beaches all the time. One regrettable failure of the landings was the difficulty of discharging LSTs because of their unwieldy size, and the presence of surf and soft sandbanks on the beaches.

After an early setback due to swell in the anchorage, and despite a moderating wind, the assault craft and troops at JOSS made a satisfactory passage ashore on each side of the small port of Licata. Those who were near the boundary of the sector 5 miles west of Licata came under heavy fire for 2 hours, and were denied any immediate reprisal because their supporting destroyers, *Swanson* and *Zoe*, had been in collision. Nevertheless, after their particularly unlucky ordeal, matters improved and 3 US Division were ashore by noon and General Truscott had set up his command post in Licata. The day was fair and warm. While engineers removed barbed wire from the beach exits and demolished pillboxes, the infantry assembled on the plains to the north and by the end of the day, 10 July, were pushing onwards to Campobello, 10 miles inland.

American troops were uniformed in olive drab trousers and shirts, and wore netted steel helmets of the same colour. Trousers were tucked inside short canvas leggings. Other gear and mess kit had been left in bags on board ship to be brought ashore later. The men carried their own weapons, ammunition, gas mask, rations, water, and a combat toilet kit.

In view of the different attitudes towards the use of naval gunfire in amphibious operations, it is interesting to hear that General Eisenhower wrote of it as 'so devastating in its effectiveness as to dispose finally of any doubts that naval guns are suitable for shore bombardment'. Certainly it was to be indispensable on D+1 (11 July), by which time German tanks were to stage a counterattack near Gela. Owing to difficulties already recounted there had been great delays in bringing

American tanks ashore on D-day. An observer of the scene at Gela that afternoon refers to landing craft coming in all along the beaches of the sea front, swelling an ever-growing, confused mass of men and trucks, overturned jeeps, wrecked boats, and a tank without a tread. In addition to this crush there was a ceaseless noise of men shouting, engines running, aircraft flying overhead, and the accompaniment of enemy gunfire from 88mm guns. On that afternoon Cunningham visited the Western Task Force, bringing with him news of the landings made by the Eastern Task Force. Desperately as the LSTs were needed ashore at Gela with their precious loads of tanks, there were too few suitable gaps in the long line of beaches into which these 2,000-ton vessels could enter to use their pontoon causeway for discharging. Moreover they were sitting ducks for bombers. LST 313 shared the fate of the destroyer *Maddox*, being hit by a bomb from an ME109. She was instantly turned into a raging inferno and suffered great loss of life as the sun set on D-day.

At daylight on 11 July the British monitor *Abercrombie* was made available to the DIME sector for the bombardment of enemy tanks reported approaching Gela, and the British cruiser *Colombo* was sent in to reinforce anti-aircraft fire in the DIME sector. The Italians had light tanks of about 10 tons. The Germans had 25-ton Mark III, and also Tiger tanks of 75 tons. There are varying reports of the number of tanks approaching (there were probably over 100 in all), but it was claimed about noon that there were thirty Tiger tanks from the Hermann Goering Panzer Division in two columns in the vicinity of Ponte Olivo, in company with troops of the Italian infantry, with more to follow. Communication difficulties delayed appropriate action by the navy, but late in the forenoon of 11 July the US 6in cruiser *Savannah* and the destroyer *Glennon* were providing accurate fire on the German tanks and Italian infantry. By 12 July order had been restored on the beaches, though still under fire, and artillery and equipment were coming ashore. The German tanks and the Italian infantry were in retreat, having lost half their numbers, and 1 US Division's front line was roughly a semi-circle of 6 miles radius, based on Gela as centre, and including well within its perimeter the airfield at Ponte Olivo. The semi-circle was steadily increasing in size.

Admiral Hall's policy at Gela was to 'support the army as far as we can shoot, where, and when the army wants it'. The tank battle on the Gela plain was regarded as a milestone in the matter of army–navy cooperation for naval gunfire support.

Eisenhower and Mountbatten called on respective commanders, 12 July, and return convoys of empty transports began to assemble.

In the JOSS sector far away at Licata to the west General Truscott had his 3 US Division firmly ashore, and was pushing rapidly northwards with 2 US Armoured Division and with the assistance of the US 6in cruisers *Birmingham* and *Brooklyn*. Menaced by bombardment from these ships and faced by Truscott's armour, the unprepared remnants of the Panzer Grenadier Division withdrew northwards.

In the CENT sector, some miles to the east, men of 45 US Division were moving north and north-east from their landings at Scoglitti and, while encountering little opposition, were intent on taking up positions on the left flank of 1 Canadian Division, which had been due to land in the vicinity of Pachino in the south-east corner of Sicily. Patton, commanding General US Seventh Army, though well pleased with the attainment of 40 miles of coastline, was anxious to push on rapidly.

The plan for the Western assault allowed for maintenance of the military forces over the beaches for a period of 30 days. The intention, as Seventh Army moved north-westwards, was to open up successively the ports of Empedocle, Marsala, Trapani, and Palermo. Meanwhile for the first 3 days of the western landings the unloading across the assault beaches at JOSS, DIME, and CENT was estimated at 66,285 personnel, 17,766 tons of equipment and stores, and 7,416 vehicles. Though Gela and Licata had been captured on the first day

of the landings, their capacity was insufficient, so that maintenance over the beaches still had to continue for several days
for the Western Task Force.

Little has been said about the excellent liaison work carried
out between the Americans and British. The following letter
by Lieut T. W. Best, RN, now Rear-Admiral, gives a brief
picture of liaison and training in connection with some British-
produced landing craft to be used in fire support.

At short notice I was sent to Djidjelli to train LCG and LCF
and establish a bombardment range at Wadi Zouar. The LCG
eventually arrived together with LCF and some LCT(R) – very
impressive craft with their salvo of 1,000 5in rockets which were
fired in about $1\frac{1}{2}$ minutes and put down a very frightening
barrage 400yd wide and 200yd deep on the beach, with a few
random rockets falling round the LCA which they followed in!

The LCG mounted two 4.7in QF guns and were designed to
get medium calibre guns close in shore to support the assaulting
troops. Unfortunately their gun direction and communications
equipment fell short of flexible requirements and they were not
easy craft to deploy. However, we persevered on the range and
got them and their largely Royal Marine crews into a state of
reasonable efficiency.

The LCF, with the exception of numbers 1 and 2, carried a
heavy armament of Oerlikon (20mm) and 2 pdr pom-poms and
were most useful in providing close range AA protection in
convoys and off the beaches. We gave them some training in
close support. LCF 1 and 2 each mounted two twin 4in HA
guns. They were excellent support ships.

After the training I went to Bizerta with four LCG and four
LCF, and joined Rear-Admiral Conolly USN in the USS
Biscayne. I helped the support craft sort out the American
Operation Orders and we did some training with the Americans
in Bizerta Lake. . . .

I sailed in *Biscayne* for the JOSS area which assaulted each
side of Licata. My job was to act as a liaison officer and assist in
controlling the British fire support craft. . . .

Strong north-west winds delayed the arrival of some landing
craft including the LCG and LCF, but we had an uneventful
passage and arrived off the beaches shortly after midnight. We
were immediately illuminated by shore searchlights and

remained so until H-hour which was, I think, about 0430, having been postponed because of late arrival of some landing craft. At the time I thought Italian shore batteries must open up at any time and shoot the sitting ducks off their shore. We were in fact very close in and within easy range – but nothing happened. The main hazard seemed to be weather and swell on the beaches and there seemed to be very little gunnery opposition. . . .

I had an immense regard for Rear-Admiral Conolly in HUSKY and was impressed by his tenacity of purpose (he was known as 'close in' Conolly), and for being so tolerant of a junior Lieut RN who was allowed to state his opinions very freely.

The following is from B. D. McPherson who, incidentally, had been one of the first to land in Dieppe in 1942:

I'm now seventy-five but still remember a bit. I was a Skipper Lieut RNR in Command of LCT 563, part of the 26th LCT Flotilla, and for HUSKY we were at Bizerta in North Africa attached to the Americans. I was loaded with 4,000 cases of petrol, smoke floats, and shells, with a few Yankee troops.

The first part of the trip was all right until we ran into a gale; the sea swept over us continually and during the night a smoke float caught fire. I got a fright so ditched them; they were too near the petrol. We beached between Licata and Gela and hadn't much trouble. The monitor *Abercrombie* together with LCGs and LCFs kept Jerry quiet, but it was mostly Italians on our sector. During daylight Jerry planes started bombing. How they survived I don't know. The flak from the American merchant ships was terrific, but Jerry did manage to hit one which was scuttled to prevent her blowing up; also a large American LCG with heavy loss of life.

There were a lot of bodies washed ashore. They were the Paratroops who had jumped over water by mistake. On the second night a lone bomber passed over us while we were on the beach and dropped a stick of bombs which straddled one of our flak ships, wounding several of her crew. Our work of unloading on the beach continued for several days.

Before leaving the western landings to see the state of affairs facing the eastern forces it is necessary to comment on two airborne assaults that were launched to carry out strategic tasks in advance of seaborne landing on the beaches. These suffered considerable casualties, especially in the second operation, and were the subject of criticism in a report made later by Cunningham. In the first of these airborne operations 3,400 men of 82 US Airborne Division were to be dropped from 226 transport planes just inland of Gela bridgehead. Unfortunately it was a latish decision, demanding a flight for which the route was east from Tunis to Malta, then north to Sicily, and then west, right along the newly established battle-front. The high winds caused some of the pilots to miss Malta, and twenty-five of them mistakenly joined a British airborne force that was flying to the Eastern assault. Cunningham reported:

> It was not until D-3 that the airborne plan became firm, and that troop-carrier command were able finally to confirm the suitability of the routes. A deserted portion of coast between the two task forces was alloted and promulgated by signal. The aircraft were to fly inland by this corridor and withdraw, passing to the north and west of Licata, well clear of the Western assault. In fact owing to heavy ground anti-aircraft fire and bad navigation, large numbers of the 226 Dakotas forsook the route and flew over the Western assault area just at the time that an enemy air raid was taking place and which was being repelled by fire from ships and from shore.

Considerable dispersion resulted, with parachutists scattered over the coastal tract of south-east Sicily from Gela to Syracuse. It took two days or more for 2,000 of these dispersed troops to reassemble at the planned dropping zone near Niscemi, 10 miles north-east of Gela. But they were able to carry out useful jobs on the way, with the purpose of frustrating the inevitable German counterattack. Though this operation had developed into a fiasco, the blow was lightened by the fact that the dispersed troops had shown so much resource in rallying among themselves and becoming a nuisance to the enemy. The Germans had two years earlier made an airborne assault on Crete, which had been only narrowly successful, and had not been repeated. But it had been carried out in daylight after a concentrated bombing assault, and there had been no severe weather and darkness to wreck the navigation.

Two nights after 82 US Airborne Division's unfortunate drop there was to be a further parachute operation for the remainder of the division. This one, like the first, was to be at night. The flight of 144 aircraft took off from Tunisia and reached the final leg of their outward journey about 10.30pm; this was roughly along the battle line of the Western assault from Sampieri, through Scoglitti and Gela, where the drop was to take place, then to Licata, where the aircraft were to turn to seaward. The transports lying off the American beaches had been under fire and repeated attacks by Axis aircraft much of that day, 11 July, and there was a renewal just as the troop-carrying aircraft arrived in the area above the Farello airfield at Gela. Many of them were hit by the concentrated anti-aircraft fire emerging from ship and shore. The sky was full of both friendly and enemy aircraft, and in spite of restrictions that had been imposed on anti-aircraft fire and information about the route and timing that had been promulgated to the ground forces, the attitude when being bombed was to treat everything as 'unfriendly'. Of the 144 troop-carrying planes that had set out in the operation twenty-three were shot down. About 100 parachutists were killed.

Misfortune in airborne landings was not confined to the Western assault, and it may be appropriate to mention in conclusion here the glider landings intended for the Eastern assault just before daylight on 10 July. For much of the following information I am grateful to the Airborne Medical Society, particularly for eyewitness accounts by some of their members. About 2,000 men of 1 British Airborne Division took off from North Africa in 137 gliders towed by Halifaxes and Dakotas on the evening of 9 July, duly protected by night fighters from Malta. The military task was to seize intact the strategic bridge of Ponte Grande, just south of Syracuse, and to hold it until 5 British Division arrived. Also taking part were members of 181 (Air Landing) Field Ambulance, who were required to be in forward positions ashore, complete with surgical teams, morphia, and anaesthetics, in preparation for treatment of the wounded.

For an hour after take-off the flight was calm. Tugs and gliders circled around to take up positions for the long flight across the Mediterranean. As the evening wore on, a strong wind blew up, setting the gliders weaving in the wake of the tugs. Pantelleria was passed and darkness fell. The landing was timed for soon after 10.00pm. The night sky was lit by bursts of flame and a searchlight picked out the approaching gliders. The tugs took avoiding action, with steep downward turns as they cast off the gliders at some 3,000ft to land. One of these gliders carried Captain G. Rigby-Jones (now MC, FRCS), a surgical team, and a hand-cart. It came to an abrupt jarring halt in collision with a stone wall and a tree, the starboard wing and the undercarriage being ripped off. But compared with some it was lucky. About half the gliders had been cast off by the tug pilots at distances varying from 2 to 10 miles from the coast. About a quarter of the troops were drowned, but a few of those who were plunged into the sea near the coast were able to struggle ashore, and some were picked up by landing craft. A platoon of the South Staffords landed near the Ponte Grande, and after a short sharp engagement captured the bridge. By 3.00pm there were increasing signs of activity as the first of the seaborne invading troops came in from the south. In the meantime the Royal Army Medical Corps had set up a regimental aid post and an advance dressing station, as well as taking part, with captured Italian automatic carbines, in the defence of this important bridge.

In connection with the glider disasters Admiral Lord Ashbourne mentions a remarkable event:

We were stopped in the *Keren* off the beaches. I saw a body floating in the sea, almost alongside and evidently alive. I told the captain of the *Keren* to pick him up. A few minutes later a dripping soldier arrived on the bridge. He turned out to be Major-General G. F. Hopkinson commanding 1 British Airborne Division. The last time I had seen him was in 1922 when I had rowed in the same boat with him at Cambridge (Caius College). We wrung out his clothes, gave him a plate of eggs and bacon, and then sent him off ashore to catch up the rest of his soldiers. Poor chap, he was later killed near Taranto 10 September 1943. He was a splendid man and must have been a great loss to his airborne troops.

I cannot refer to these accounts of airborne operations without mentioning one letter I received from a soldier who could see humour as well as tragedy. He yelled out to a group of struggling men in the sea near a ditched glider, 'Who are you?' Came the answer, 'We're airborne!'

With particular reference to the employment of airborne troops, which was still relatively novel, Cunningham wrote:

In the initial planning great weight was lent to the value of airborne troops for the softening of beach defences. The conditions of light required for the employment of paratroops were inimical to the secure and undetected approach of naval forces. In view of the importance attached to the airborne attack, the date selected for the assault was one which was not favourable from the naval point of view. In fact the airborne troops were never used in the manner projected, but that they were not to be so used did not emerge until it was too late to change the date. In consequence the navies, for no advantage, had to accept a disadvantageous light for approach, and a subsequent period of moonlight nights off the beaches which could otherwise have been avoided.

A seaborne assault is unalterably committed to a date for some days in advance of D-day. It may well be that, on the selected date, airborne troops are weather-bound and cannot operate. It does, therefore, appear more necessary that airborne troops should be considered as a useful auxiliary rather than as a governing factor.

The commander of the Western assault, Vice-Admiral Hewitt, gave a very long and detailed report after the landings, much of which made particular reference to the United States Naval, Military, and Air organisations. It was frankly critical of shortcomings and deficiencies, but gave credit where due:

Unique in many respects, the most impressive fact was the vast scale upon which the operation was launched. The relentless vigour with which the assault was pressed home, regardless of loss or difficulty, merits the highest praise. The initiative, perseverance, and loyalty of the officers and men comprising the Western Task Force is acknowledged with pleasure. The co-operation manifested between the army and navy and the comradeship and combat efficiency demonstrated by units of the Royal Navy and the United States Navy in joint action against a common foe presages the ultimate victory of the Allied Nations.

8 Eastern Assault

We have seen in the previous chapter that US Seventh Army had successfully landed on the western beaches, under the direction of Admiral Hewitt, in spite of unfavourable weather, beach hazards, and sporadic opposition, and were already advancing northward into Sicily. Meanwhile at noon, 9 July, Admiral Ramsay had assumed operational control of all ships and craft taking part in the Eastern assault, and had sailed from Malta in the headquarters ship *Antwerp* to witness the concentration of big ship convoys from the Middle East and the United Kingdom, and their junction with the groups of landing craft from Sfax, Tripoli, and Malta, all destined for the south-east corner of Sicily.

A glance at Map 2 will remind us of the disposition of the various groups in the Eastern Task Force, attacking the south-east while the Western Task Force was assaulting the Licata, Gela, and Scoglitti beaches. We may recall, north to south, on the eastern front (from Syracuse to the Pachino peninsula), the division into three groups: Force A under the command of Rear-Admiral Troubridge, with the task of landing 5 British Division and 50 Division in the region of Avola and Cassibile, ACID North sector, the early capture of Syracuse being the prime objective; Force B under the command of Rear-Admiral McGrigor with the task of landing 51 Highland Division at Portopalo Bay in the Pachino peninsula, BARK South sector; and Force V under the command of Rear-Admiral Vian with the task of landing 1 Canadian Division plus 40 and 41 Royal Marine Commando in the BARK West sector. In addition,

British destroyer on LST's quarter, off Cape Passero (LJS)

in BARK East sector under Captain Lord Ashbourne, 231 Brigade was to be landed at Marzamemi.

The great mass of ships and craft were to proceed after their rendezvous off Malta to their respective release positions, shown in Map 2. They included great liners, one of which, the *Reina del Pacifico*, we shall later follow in detail for a while. There were large ships such as the *Duchess of Bedford, Monarch of Bermuda, Winchester Castle, Keren, Strathnaver, Otranto,* and medium and smaller ships of every variety. The fast convoys were to arrive first, at midnight, immediately followed by gun support craft and tank landing craft. Then would come the slower convoys and finally the tank landing ships. Close gunfire support for the military forces was provided during the assaults on D-day by British ships – the monitors *Roberts* and *Erebus,* the cruisers *Newfoundland, Orion, Mauritius,* and *Uganda* of Force K, together with the destroyers *Eskimo, Nubian, Tartar, Laforey, Loyal,* and *Lookout.*

The main fleet covering force previously mentioned concentrated in a position 240 miles east of Malta at 9.00pm on the day before D-day (see Map 3), having detached the cruisers *Aurora* and *Penelope* with two destroyers to bombard Catania and Taormina and to secure the exposed northerly flank of the Eastern assault. Meanwhile Force Z, consisting of the battleships *Howe* and *King George V*, proceeded 9 July to create a diversion off eastern Sicily and to bombard the western ports of Trapani and Marsala.

As has been described, the weather deteriorated suddenly and the wind freshened on 9 July sufficiently to put many of the plans in jeopardy, and although a welcome moderation arrived for D-day, the swell and surf were an upsetting factor for the American landings on the exposed south-west coast. The Eastern assault by the British, however, had the benefit of some protection in the lee of the land.

It would take too long to give a blow by blow account of the various movements and actions on the beaches. It is proposed, therefore, broadly to cover the main movements, and add a few selected extracts from some of those who witnessed the events and played their part in the operation. There were many points of common interest, and it is valuable to have the individual points of view from some of those many thousands who took part in the assault on Sicily.

Lieut Anthony Daniell was captain of the submarine *Unison* at the Force B release position in sector BARK South, where 51 Division were to land 7 miles off Portopalo Bay in the Pachino peninsula (Map 2). He writes:

We had to fix our position accurately on the day previous to D-day, and bottom in our allotted position having laid a sonar buoy to seaward. We then surfaced soon after midnight, still in position, of course.

91

One tragic thing I remember clearly was seeing gliders coming down in the sea a mile or two away, and my taking the decision that we mustn't move to look for survivors in case we misled the approaching convoy.

We carried an infra-red light that we flashed on the reciprocal of the approach course. The theory was that the motor launch which led the convoy would pick up our infra-red transmissions with suitable receivers. However, a fresh breeze had got up from northward and the motor launches couldn't keep up. Our first sighting of our convoy was in the shape of a minesweeper (very close). It was too late to make recognition signals, which anyway might have alerted the enemy, and so I strung together as many short Anglo-Saxon words as I could think of and got the reply in suitably phrased Scots.

The really memorable thing for us was to see, as dawn broke, all the liners and other shipping lying at anchor in what since the end of 1940 had been such dangerous waters.

Three or four miles west of 51 Division's landing beaches were those for 1 Canadian Division in BARK West sector. Admiral C. R. L. Parry, then a captain, stresses the widespread suspense:

The 21st Destroyer Flotilla, of which I was Captain (D), had escorted KMF 18 carrying 1 Canadian Division from Liverpool, and after fuelling at Malta sailed in the late afternoon of 9 July 1943 to rendezvous with this convoy for the early stages of Operation HUSKY. The weather was fine but with a north-westerly wind and nasty lop. This caused much discomfort to the landing craft as we passed them on our way to take up our position at the head of the destroyer screen to port of Admiral Vian's flagship *Hilary* and the troopships in which the Canadians were embarked in Force V.

The scene towards sunset was impressive to a degree, the sea to the west of Gozo covered with ships of every size steaming towards their allotted positions, ours being the beaches of BARK West.

At the appropriate moment a blue signalling light was seen on the port bow, this being from the submarine *Unrivalled*, marking vessel for the release position. Ahead, over the dark enemy-held coast, could be seen the flashes of exploding bombs and some gunfire, but all well inland. This steady approach towards a hostile shore with all its unknown uncertainties was one of the most memorable events that I have ever known. What was to come was a matter of conjecture but at least we knew that nothing had been left to chance in the planning of such an enterprise never before attempted.

Some 17 miles northwards of the *Unison* and the *Unrivalled* was the submarine *Unruffled*, marking the Force A release position for the convoy transporting, among others, 5 Division. I have a letter giving a 'worm's eye view', as he calls it, written by Captain R. D. Butt, who at the time of HUSKY was a nineteen-year-old midshipman. It is useful to get a glimpse of his experience. He had been given the command of a sub-division of three assault landing craft, led from LCA 275, and carried in the ex-liner *Reina del Pacifico*. He had for his crew a coxswain, sternsheetman, Lewis gunner, and a 'dear old man aged thirty' who looked after the craft's petrol engines 'with loving care'. It is interesting to follow his movements at the end of the customary period of training, day and night, which in his case took place in Aqaba in the Gulf of Suez, while others were rehearsing in places as far away as the Clyde in Scotland. He writes:

At Aqaba a full scale replica of the beach defences south of Syracuse, though we did not then know its identity, had been built, and we carried out a full scale practice assault on a brigade front, including landing armour and vehicles. For the dress rehearsal a good deal of ammunition and demolition charges were expended.

In one of the very rare errors that branch ever commits, the Hydrographer's Office in Cairo had produced chartlets for the rehearsal on which the longitude scale was over a mile in error, and this threw the landing into some confusion. It proved a blessing in disguise because on the night of the actual assault on Sicily we were thrown into a somewhat similar disarray by the weather, and our experience at Aqaba helped a lot.

A couple of days before we were due to sail from Port Said we found the place decked with green flags as the local populace seemed certain that we were to liberate Greece. We did not know our actual destination and were incensed when one of the operations staff had left the operations room unlocked with a marked-up map of Greece visible, through the door. We felt this a gross breach of security risking the success of the operation. The staff were ostracised until some days after we had sailed and had been briefed, and realised that this was a well thought out cover plan.

It was a fine sight to see our force of ex-liners manoeuvring in close formation like a squadron of well drilled cruisers. We had a small close escort and a heavy covering force well to the north keeping the Italians in harbour.

On the afternoon before D-day it began to blow a near gale. Even in the *Reina* the soldiers were seasick, and in the lightly loaded vessels that had joined us from North African ports, and which were to come alongside us for their troops, there was rolling up to 45° each side.

We were given a tot of rum at dinner time before the final approach to ACID North sector, and tried to get some sleep. Everyone was a bit tensed although confident of success. I remember seeking out the Battalion Commander of the King's Own Yorkshire Light Infantry and the ex-bank manager Company Commander whom I was to land from my boat, and warn them that the deterioration made the risk of a disorderly landing probable. They took it calmly and expressed confidence that the Navy would do all that was possible.

The plan was that our Force A should land 5 Division over the beaches between C. Murro di Porco, just south of Syracuse, and the town of Avola. The liners were to heave to and launch the LCA from about 10 miles offshore in order to avoid artillery, mines, and detection. The LCA would be led to a position about a mile offshore by motor launches specially converted, and then be released in waves 15 minutes apart.

That evening I was sitting aft in the *Reina* listening to HLI pipers playing warlike music at dusk when the summit of Mount Etna appeared on the horizon. We felt naked. If we could see land, then an observer there must see us.

Our landing craft were slung from the ship's lifeboat davits, but were much longer than the normal lifeboats for which the davits were designed. Hence they had to be secured in two tiers overlapping. There was no disengaging gear, and the single wire falls terminated in a vast hook which had to be unhooked from

Life preservers at the ready as LST 65 approaches Sicily (LJS)

a steel ring at each end of the boat. With the craft rising and
falling several feet in the middle of the night and with about
thirty-three fully armed soldiers on board each one, launching
and disengagement was an alarming operation with every risk
of severed fingers or cracked skulls. Furthermore any delay in
unhooking a boat in the lower tier would hold up two craft in

95

the upper tier. To my relief LCA 275 achieved a faultless launch and we proceeded about 400yd ahead of *Reina* at slow speed to await the rest.

Soon we were shipping seas green over the bow-ramp and had to reduce speed to 3 knots with about 18in of water milling about in the bottom of the boat. After considerable and prolonged doubt about our position we sighted the folbot marking the beach adjacent to our proper one, but as it was beginning to get light and we had already attracted the attention of an Italian machine gun, the Company Commander asked to be landed at once, although we were about a mile too far towards Avola.

The craft grounded a few yards offshore due to the amount of water we had shipped. The soldiers waded in single file ashore behind the officer, fortunately on dead ground that Italian opposition could not reach from their gun emplacements. We then heard a few shots and screams away to the left, followed by cheers and the skirl of the bagpipes, and knew that the HLI had hit their target, and our chaps were not alone.

LST 65, with skipper Lieut L. J. Smith in foreground (LJS)

The touchdown in .the ACID Sector was only 10 minutes short of the planned time, but many landing craft in Force A, as in Butt's case, went to the wrong beach. Landing in a craft at the north end of this sector was J. C. E. Eldridge, then a captain RASC, shortly to be transferred to RE, who also met problems after disembarking, in his case from the *Duchess of Bedford*. He writes:

On the morning of the landings we were sitting at breakfast on board prior to climbing down scramble nets into assault craft to land on Red Beach at Cassibile, and eating our first kippers for three years, when the ship's radio brought us news that successful landings had taken place on Sicily and were advancing without opposition towards Syracuse.

In fact, since we were to be just about the very first ashore, and long before the Yanks, and the operation had been delayed a little by bad weather, the announcement seemed premature, especially as German 88mm guns were firing towards us from the hills behind the olive groves, and the *Warspite* was lobbing salvoes in return; to say nothing of the numerous Stuka and Heinkel raids we were to suffer.

One thing remains in my memory. There had been much speculation as to whether a desperate use of gas would be attempted by the enemy. During the hot afternoon of that day one or two of us were walking through the olive groves during a minor bombing. Suddenly there was a strong unidentified smell, and the gas alarm was given. Fortunately, when we later emerged from our respirators it was found to be only a strong concentration of local herbage – mostly wild thyme – disturbed by the bombs.

I remember a personal dilemma. We had to sleep in the rocky hinterland behind the beach. There was no chance of digging foxholes, for there was little earth and much rock. So I constructed a coffin-type shell of rocks around me. Fine, but there was of course no protection from above, and enemy planes were still coming over, and bits of shell casings were still dropping. My problem was how best to utilise my steel helmet, and I remember deciding that I would prefer something through my head rather than elsewhere and consequently spent the night with my helmet over the pit of my stomach!

Brief spell after unloading LST 65 (LJS)

One of the supporting ships for Force A in the approach to Sicily was the destroyer *Rockwood*, whose captain, Lieut Lombard-Hobson, remarked that the Mediterranean seemed alive with ships and craft of all types and sizes and it was surprising that by 8.30pm, when they were only 30 miles off Sicily, there was no sign of the enemy in any form, and the chief menace was the strong wind which delayed arrival and caused confusion and doubt. He wrote in his report:

Opposition ashore seemed very slight and it appeared as though the force had achieved the impossible in complete tactical as well as strategical surprise. One long range searchlight at Cape Passero carried out a slow routine sweep to seaward, but just as it was coming on to the assembled forces, it dipped and went out. Later, another searchlight swept round and in its beam firmly held *Rockwood* and *Eskimo* at the head of Group III. But this likewise went out, having either seen nothing or having been appalled at what it had seen.

As dawn broke, success signals were sent up from several beaches. I proceeded along the coast to look for batteries and machine-gun posts that might be menacing our troops. Two were seen engaging landing craft and I opened a direct bombardment against them. They were soon silenced.

B. O. Mitchenor, who had arrived in the Middle East as one of 15,000 passengers in the *Queen Mary*, and was to land at Cassibile with Force A, speaks favourably of the training period at Kabrit on the Bitter Lakes, where in addition to gaining experience in landing on beaches, he was taught the skill of using roller runways for the landing of stores. He then comments on the method of memorising beach details and geographical features:

After stopping at Port Said for a route march and bathe, the convoy proceeded to assemble at Alexandria before setting off down the Mediterranean for an unknown destination, which was soon to become apparent to us when we were taken in groups to the bowels of the ship and shown a built up model of the beach in Sicily where we were to land. Every possible point of interest on that beach was shown, including gun emplacements, minefields, assembly areas, etc., and this was a great feature of all the detailed planning which went into this operation.

At about 1am on 10 July, with some of my troop, I entered our LCA. We were lowered down the side of the ship. We proceeded shorewards with Sicily well lit by fires from the continuous bombing it had received for several days. Our orders were to wait until a green light had gone up telling us that a commando had taken the beach, and then to land. At that time we were seven miles out from the island, and it took some time for us to approach the shore. My LCA ended up stuck in a sandbank and the occupants, including myself, were forced to wade ashore with the sea up to our armpits.

About 12 miles south of the ACID North objectives of

Avola and Cassibile was Marzamemi in sector BARK East, which was the destination of Captain Lord Ashbourne's force carrying 231 Brigade. It was called the Malta Brigade because it was originally stationed in that island before transferring to Egypt for HUSKY training. The brigade's task was to build up a bridgehead and an area for stores. Chaplain Denis Tollet, with 1 Battalion the Dorset Regiment, writes:

> Our invasion ship was the SS *Strathnaver* and after the briefing on board I well remember the doubts about the timing of the invasion owing to the dull and misty weather. However it was 'on' and each man received a stiff tot of rum before climbing down the side of the ship on the ropes into the LST. There was desultory enemy bombing, one bomb landing amongst us but failing to explode! At daylight we immediately pushed inland with little opposition, the Italians surrendering almost on sight, though a few needed dealing with. It was not until we got further inland and came up against the Jerries that serious fighting began. There were very few casualties until then.

Also with 231 Brigade was Michael Aldworth, now major, a Royal Marine officer of 7 Battalion RM who writes (among other matters) of opportunities that may suddenly come one's way – in his case, a locomotive.

> In due course, we were allocated as the Beach Group for 231 Brigade, a first-rate Army formation consisting of 1 Hampshires, 1 Dorsets, and 2 Devons, whose role was to make a landing and beach-head at the village of Marzamemi on the south-east corner of Sicily. Operation HUSKY began for us on the last day in June when we embarked in the three ships *Keren*, *Strathnaver*, and *Otranto* at Suez, and then steamed up the Canal and past our old 'home' at Kabrit.
> You will of course be aware of the excellent Staff work which assembled convoys from all over the world and martialled them in meticulous order for the final run-in. The weather had deteriorated, but this of course did not affect our big ships and on the evening of 9 July, I remember looking ahead of the ship at the great mass of Mount Etna, looming up in the evening sky, and wondering whether any of the opposition were

sitting on the top with field glasses and watching us approach.

We had been told two facts about Marzamemi – firstly, that in the village there was a wine 'factory' (for want of a better word) with a tall chimney (useful as a leading mark); and secondly, that a house on an island 100yd offshore was owned by an Italian professor who had a beautiful daughter! Needless to say, neither professor nor daughter were in residence! [Lord Ashbourne took over this house for use as his headquarters when he disembarked from the *Keren*.]

At 0245 on 10 July the assault flights of landing craft left the ships and by 0400 the Hampshires and Dorsets had with great professionalism cleared the beaches and were pushing inland towards a coastal battery, aided when daylight came by fire from the Dutch gunboats, *Flores* and *Soemba*. Opposition was light, and even the coastal battery soon gave up. *Strathnaver* steamed closer inshore and my Company eventually landed in broad daylight, taking up a defensive position on the right flank of the beach-head, whence a counter-attack might be expected. One was indeed mounted in the afternoon by French M35 tanks manned by Italians from Rosolini, but was broken up by A/T guns and Sherman tanks before it reached us.

I was ordered to take a patrol up the railway line on our left flank to the town of Pachino, to see if there were any sign of the Canadians who had landed round the corner to our left. There were no signs of the Canadians, but what I did find in the station yard was a wonderful great steam locomotive with a train of empty trucks and the Italian crew just waiting for someone to tell them what to do. We told them to raise steam, which took a long time (during which OC 'B' Company turned up, closely followed by a full colonel in the Army who told him to get back to his company but allowed me to continue raising steam. Poor OC 'B' Company was to be killed on 20 July). However, eventually we backed the locomotive on to the train and with myself on the front buffer beam spotting for mines on the track, we made our slow and stately way to Marzamemi station where we dropped the train and took the engine on to our platoon position! I think I can claim to have run the first train in liberated Europe!

The Marzamemi area was the scene of a good deal of bombing from the air because it was of course being used as a build-up area for stores. One Macchi 202 – their single seat fighter – made a dead set at me, so I drew my elderly .455 revolver, aimed at the pilot's head outlined against the sky and fired at him, being able to see the bullets going up and making the necessary corrections. He crashed, but as two cruisers, four destroyers, one heavy and one light AA Regiment were all firing at him, I didn't claim him as my bird!

The passage of Force B to the BARK South sector merits some attention. This was largely a shore to shore assault in which the bulk of the troops would have to live on board landing craft under cramped conditions during the passage. To reduce this time as much as possible, a large number of loaded LCIs (L) started from Malta with convoy SBF 2 on the afternoon before D-day. They had bunks for 200 fully equipped troops and initially sailed from Sfax. The task was to transport 51 Highland Division to BARK South, where they were to land and capture the town and airfield of Pachino. They were also to link with 1 Canadian Division, who were landing on their left flank, and then to advance inland to capture various towns and the railway.

The force comprised four cross-channel ships – *Royal Ulsterman*, *Royal Scotsman*, *Queen Emma*, and *Princess Beatrix* – carrying twenty-seven landing craft. There were also twenty-eight tank-landing ships, with twenty-eight tank-landing craft and thirty-six infantry-landing craft. One of the tank-landing ships, LST 429, was lost by fire during passage but there were no casualties among the troops. The times of sailing of the four convoys SBF 1, SBF 2, SBS 1, and SBM 1 in Force B, all under Rear-Admiral McGrigor in the headquarters ship *Largs*, were arranged with the intention that the convoys should reach the release position $2\frac{1}{2}$ hours before H-hour. *Hunt*-class destroyers and motor launches were in close support, and minesweepers swept the channel ahead.

The shore to shore policy to be carried out for a large portion of Force B compelled craft to sail under sea conditions that were almost too much for them. The tank landing craft LCT 547 capsized with the loss of six Sherman tanks. Several

In the wake of LCI 122; nonchalance before the assault (SCG)

of the LCTs broke down and had to be taken in tow, and it became necessary to reduce speed to prevent the LCIs from being left behind. By an alteration of course it was possible to take a short cut to the release position, and the main convoy was only 15 minutes late. Even so, most of the LCTs in particular reached that position some 2 hours adrift. It was considered, however, that the force had been undetected so far. Moreover there had been a marked improvement in sea conditions, apart from a heavy swell, as the force approached the lee of the land. On reaching the release positions half an hour after midnight, the force was able to lower LCAs fully manned in 6 minutes. A first-hand report of conditions in SBF 1 of Force B comes from H. Ian Tait who, since he was taking passage in the *Royal Ulsterman*, was spared the rigours of the many hours of confinement suffered by the shore to shore troops. He was then a twenty-year-old soldier in the intelligence section of 7 Argyll and Sutherland Highlanders, 154 Brigade, 51 Highland Division. He writes:

Wet landing on rocky beach, 10 July 1943

Late on the night of 9 July we transferred to LCAs and LCIs for the actual assault. At the time of the transfer the seas were running so high that it was not possible to utilise the scrambling nets on the ship's side to board the assault craft, and the transfer was effected by soldiers jumping individually, as the assault vessels rose to the deck level of the troop-ship. Unfortunately, I mistimed my jump and started to fall between the two vessels, but was arrested in my downward plunge by Captain I. C. Cameron, who grabbed me by the rim of my steel helmet and pulled me back on the deck of the troop-ship. My second attempt at transfer was more successful.

The vessel in which we made the run in to the beach was an LCI and, as far as I can recollect, it had some sort of accommodation with canvas bunks in tiers of three, and we were quartered in this accommodation. We were issued with a rum ration, and such was the intensity of the storm that most of my colleagues were seasick. Our landing point was on a beach near Portopalo on the extreme south-east tip of the island and the Intelligence Reports which we had read earlier stated that since Sicilians had been seen bathing from the beach, it was considered to be unmined and unwired. My later observations of the inhabitants of that area indicated that most of them had never had a bath, far less a bathe in the sea!

Our forward companies landed at 2.45am on the morning of 10 July, and slight resistance was met; our only casualties were wounded by a grenade thrown into their LCA as they were disembarking. The skipper of our LCI refused to run the vessel on to the beach, as he was worried in case he could not get it off again and we were consequently dropped off in what was probably 8ft of water. Since neither of the landing ramps on either side of the bow would operate, all the troops on the vessel had to go over the side on ropes and pull themselves hand-over-hand on a rope line which a volunteer hauled on to the shore and made secure to some object there.

The beachhead was easily consolidated and most of the Italian coastal troops either gave things up or retreated into the interior. Soon after we landed we were greeted by a Sicilian peasant who came along dispensing wine from a cask on the back of a mule, and this was probably the first time most of us had drunk wine for breakfast.

The following few days were a case of marching in pursuit of the elusive enemy since there was virtually no resistance

until we reached Buccheri. On 13 July 231 Brigade had unsuc-
cessfully attacked two hills near the village which were held by
the Germans, and our brigade was ordered to take Buccheri
on the night of 14 July. The start line was about 1½ miles from
the objective and the attack was launched at about 10pm but
we encountered no resistance, and the only problem during the
advance was the extremely broken country that we had to cross;
this consisted of numerous olive groves divided by stone walls.
For the next few days we marched north against increasing
opposition until we eventually ran into the main Axis defence
line, south of Mount Etna. It appeared that the main strong
point in the line was Gerbini Airfield, and our battalion was to
attack and capture the airfield on the night of 20/21 July.

John Whitfield of the Royal Engineers took passage in LST
8, destined to land at a beach in the south-east corner. He
speaks of a 'few very dirty days waterproofing a variety of
vehicles'. Waterproofing the DUKWs was unnecessary, since
they were designed to travel on sea or land. But the average

LST 407 and LCM 81–14 (SCG)

LCA 492 in foreground and LCI in middle distance beyond (SCG)

truck or vehicle disembarking from landing craft or landing ship was almost bound to be exposed to considerable amounts of water. Occasionally they sank into the water gap between ramp and beach. Hence there were strict orders that de-waterproofing must be carried out at the earliest opportunity. This meant removing the 'breathers' that had been fitted to brakes, crank-case, clutch, axle, distributor, and dynamo when initially waterproofed. Whitfield writes:

There is little doubt that after the rough sea passage the average soldier, of any rank, wished only to have his feet on solid land once again, irrespective of enemy opposition. For that reason there was not a great deal of fear concerning the landing. Certainly very little opposition was encountered in the Cape Passero area and it was not till later that we came up against strong resistance from the Germans when we were attempting to get possession of the numerous air strips on the Gerbini plain south of Catania.

108

Whitfield comments on a soldier's guide which, among the useful phrases, contained the bizarre remark one was likely to hear often: 'Non sparate siamo amici', which, translated, means 'Don't shoot, we are friends'. Whitfield describes his arrival:

The landing ship suddenly grounded heavily and stopped. The huge doors opened and the ramp began to descend, finally falling into the water with a considerable splash. There was considerable activity on the beach and I could see tanks and infantry moving inland. A naval officer roared at me to get my vehicle moving. I engaged gear and moved down the ramp. Assuming there was about 2–3ft of water, I put my foot down on the accelerator. We plunged off the ramp and sank gracefully into some 8ft of water on the shore side of an unmarked sand bank.

There was a great deal of shouting and waving and we found ourselves standing on the sand bank up to our waists in water as the LST backed off and moved further down the beach where it found a gap and drove on to the beach proper. Meanwhile a D8 bulldozer backed into the water quite close to us, and unwound one of its cables. By dint of diving we attached this to our vehicle. There was a slight delay as we crouched in the water while an Italian plane strafed the beach and then we were dragged on to dry land. The Captain had a flask of brandy which he considerately offered to me. With luck, the help of some REME mechanics, and good waterproofing, we soon had the engine started and drove up off the beach. It was by now intensely hot and we rapidly dried out.

We have covered the various incidents described by some of those members of the Eastern assault who landed on the eastern beaches extending from ACID North to BARK South, and we come finally to the destination of Force V under Rear-Admiral Vian in the *Hilary*. His force was organised in the United Kingdom and embarked in convoys KMF 18 and KMS 18, carrying 1 Canadian Division and Royal Marine Commandos 40 and 41, all due to land near Punta di Formiche in sector BARK West. Their task was to protect the left flank of 51 Division, and with them to capture the airfield at Pachino, and advance inland towards the north-west.

Convoy KMS 18 was unlucky in losing three military transport store ships – the *City of Venice* and the *Saint Essylt* on 4 July, and the *Devis*, which was carrying the commodore (Rear-Admiral England), on 5 July. All three were sunk by U-boat, and were three of the only four ships to be lost in all the many ships of all the convoys before the assault began. The official report says, 'The *Devis* was abandoned in orderly fashion'. Nevertheless it is interesting to hear what the commodore had to say about it:

It was my privilege to be asked by Admiral Vian to be commodore of his assault convoy. All went well until the convoy reached the Mediterranean where we had a strong escort of eight destroyers. Shortly after passing Algiers *Devis* was sunk by what I calculated was more than one torpedo and we lost a large number of Canadian troops we were carrying. We received no warning of the U-boat attack. This I put down to the fact the destroyers had been employed solely in the Atlantic and had no experience of working Asdics in the denser water in the Mediterranean.

It was obvious from the moment we were hit that *Devis* would not stay afloat for long, and after sending my assistant round the upper deck to make sure that everyone who was able to had abandoned ship, I found myself on the focsle with the master who then insisted he must be the last to leave. Actually we slid down a grass line together, with the bows of the ship rising rapidly and the stern awash. So honour was satisfied, and together we watched the ship go down. We were picked up by a destroyer which after landing survivors at Bougie took me to rejoin the convoy. Approaching the swept channel round Cape Bon our escort was reinforced by Commodore Agnew's squadron of cruisers *Aurora*, *Penelope*, *Cleopatra*, *Euryalus*, *Sirius*, and *Dido* and we hoped most of our troubles were over.

The rest of the passage of the convoy to Sicily passed without incident, and our main apprehension was the deteriorating weather and the freshening wind. As we approached the Malta channel we received a great boost to our morale when sighting many other convoys converging on their objectives.

Ambulances driving ashore over pontoon of empty tanks (SCG)

Intelligence reports of runnels on the beaches of BARK West led to the preparation of alternative plans ordering the use of LCAs if the LCTs should fail to arrive. This caused confusion, especially when the LCT group was delayed by swell and the transfer of troops from ship to landing craft became difficult. Nevertheless the first flight formed up and moved off at 3.15am, finding their beach without great difficulty, thanks to the folbot. They touched down at 4.55am and with fire support craft were able to subdue the slight machine-gun opposition ashore. As soon as the channel was reported swept at 4.25am the *Hilary* and the 15in monitor *Roberts* moved to an anchorage closer inshore. Fire from batteries was countered by bombardment from the *Roberts* and the destroyers *Blankney* and *Puckeridge*, and ceased at 6.00am. By nightfall on D-day empty ships were being sent to Malta and Tripoli under escort. That same afternoon the fast minelayer HMS *Abdiel* passed through

LCT unloading near Avola; LCM right foreground (SCG)

BARK West carrying Admiral Cunningham on a tour of inspection.

The shallow nature of the beaches in BARK West and the ever-shifting sandbanks proved a great obstacle and it was therefore decided on D+1 to close them and to concentrate unloading at BARK South. There were so many vessels unable to reach the shore effectively in BARK West, that a considerable amount of unloading was done by DUKWs. Richard Evans, who was a driver and saw the scene at BARK West, says:

We landed without incident and deposited our cargoes at dumps a short distance inland. This of course was the all important role of the DUKWs as supplies were taken straight through, thus avoiding handling and congestion on the small beaches. There was considerable air attack going on; but we had fighter cover from Malta to deal with it reasonably effectively. I was driving the sixth DUKW to leave the LST, as our platoons were divided into sections of six vehicles.

The situation was pretty unique as we had to adapt ourselves

112

from motor transport drivers to boat crews who knew how to tie up alongside merchant ships and load our craft from derricks, often in quite a heavy swell, and having to climb rope ladders to the decks of ships and return by these to our amphibians. Back on the beach we had to revert to land-handling, until we returned empty and into the sea for another load. This could become confusing when one was tired, and I know that all of us at some time stood on the brake pedal when approaching the side of the ship at too great a speed, instead of going hard astern.

The actual landings in Sicily had been, as far as the troops were concerned, in many cases an anticlimax. Preparations had been made for tough opposition and a large number of casualties, but resistance on the whole had so far been slight. The following account from Group-Captain F. H. L. Searl treats the occasion as if it were a picnic; but his reference to ULTRA is informative and it is also intriguing to read something about the Mafia:

I commanded a small unit of Advanced Air Headquarters of the Desert Air Force that had supported Eighth Army through the western desert operations. On the night before the invasion I had a very comfortable dinner at the Union Club in Malta and drove down in my jeep to be the last aboard one of the tank landing vessels, so that I could be the first one ashore.

When I got on board a Marine took me to my cabin (with fresh white sheets) and gravely told me that the invasion was timed for 4 o'clock the next morning and what time would I like my early morning tea?

So I went ashore after a hot shower and with a good breakfast under my belt, just at first light. Together with my corporal driver (and his dog) we drove ashore without any signs of resistance. I was not surprised at this because I had known through ULTRA sources that many German troops had been withdrawn from the island and that the German High Command was highly suspicious of an Italian capitulation. We located the site of the first airfield, which was to be levelled out by the sappers, who were already on the scene. When I judged it ready we had to be in radio touch with Malta to order aircraft

LCT 379 unloading vehicles over rectangular tank pontoon (SCG)

off the ground and into Sicily; there was clearly nothing to be done for at least a couple of hours, so after establishing radio touch with Malta to see that the transmitter/receiver was working, we decided to go for a quiet drive around the neighbourhood.

One of the first things we noticed was a number of what were apparently anti-aircraft gun barrels sticking up from a quarry and we consequently drove over to see what was going on. Precisely nothing: a dispirited Italian unit, under the command of a lieutenant, was sitting around doing nothing very much and obviously very anxious not to become entangled in any kind of shooting war. The Italian officer spoke a little French and after something of an awkward pause he decided that he ought to hand over his automatic pistol to me, a point which I had not considered. I then told him that his men should pile arms and he asked me then, having surrendered, what he should do about it. I told him that probably the best thing was to stay put and perhaps hang out a white flag if he had anything suitable around to make one from. After another awkward pause he asked me if we would like some coffee, which turned out to be the genuine article and not German ersatz. There seemed to be little else that we could do about it;

we drank our coffee and moved on to encounter a rather mysterious American officer with an Italian name who had been attached to us for some time. After a little conversation it became quite clear that he was a member of the Mafia and this was his sole reason for being dressed as a captain in the American army. He had come ashore much earlier from a tank landing craft further up the coast and had already made some of his local contacts with his Mafia friends. As evidence of this he had a large jar of grappa with which he had been presented by his Sicilian Mafia friends and we parted with mutual expressions of esteem.

Our aircraft flew in during the early afternoon and there was at no stage any hostile air action or even reconnaissance. The parachute drop further north had gone badly wrong and the casualties there were extremely heavy because the paratroops carried in American aircraft had been told to jump when in fact the aircraft were well out to sea. There was only one major air operation of which we had foreknowledge, again through ULTRA sources, and we were able to get most of the aircraft off the ground before the German attack came in. However, some fuel dumps were set afire and we confidently expected that there would be a follow-up during the night, since we were at some disadvantage. However, no attempt of any sort was made.

There is a further story about the Mafia from Geoffrey Sterne of 78 Division. He refers to the time when the Hermann Goering Division was effectually holding up the British Eighth Army on the plain of Catania. At that time the American Seventh Army suddenly seemed to have got over its earlier setbacks and delays with an accelerating push. Sterne writes:

The Americans landed west of us on the south coast with targets Palermo et al. They achieved their targets in double quick time, to our amazement. There appeared to be no opposition. We had assumed that the German decision to withdraw eastwards was to avoid being cut off by the British. I heard the story about a year ago.

Before the war our American friends had great problems in USA with Mafia gangsters, and found that the only way to 'get' them was through their non-payment of taxes. Consequently,

LCM (left) *and LCT* (middle) *about to beach off Avola* (SCG)

at the beginning of the war there were several of these gangsters in prison serving long sentences. When it was planned that US forces would take part in the invasion of Sicily, it was also recalled that Sicily was the home of the Mafia. Research showed that one of the imprisoned gangsters had a brother living in Sicily who was a very influential Mafia person. The Americans approached this Mafia gangster prisoner and said that, if he would contact his brother in Sicily and it could be arranged that the Germans would be so harassed that there would virtually be no opposition to the US forces, he would be released with a free pardon. They undertook to deliver such a letter.

The letter was written, and delivered, and the brother did his part, which explains a lot. Unfortunately it didn't apply to our British Eighth Army front.

In a raid a force achieves its objective, then re-embarks and withdraws. But in this great invasion the landing was only the beginning, however difficult and costly, with the necessity for a swift and increasing follow-up. For this reason landing ships as well as certain craft were sent back to Malta and North

116

Africa as soon as they had unloaded. Many thereby escaped the enemy air attacks, which began with a raid on the beaches by four FW190s at 1.15pm on 10 July, followed at 4.30pm by attacks by Ju88s on what shipping was left in the anchorages. The hospital ship *Talamba*, fully lighted, lying 5 miles to seaward in ACID area, and awaiting the arrival of wounded casualties, was deliberately bombed and sunk with considerable loss of life. *Talamba*, however, was the only ship sunk on this occasion, and thereafter hospital ships were ordered to lie further offshore and to darken ship. During daylight enemy aircraft were kept off by Allied fighters. After dark, smokescreens and Allied night fighters proved to be effectual in reducing casualties in harbours and anchorages. The port of Syracuse fell to British soldiers before nightfall on 10 July, as promised by General Montgomery. It seemed to be a good omen.

Let us now return to Admiral Sir Bertram Ramsay who was so greatly responsible for the HUSKY planning from the earliest stages. The following comments are extracts from his report of proceedings of the Eastern Task Force:

> Valuable experience was gained, notably in regard to maintenance through the beaches, opening of captured ports, and naval support of the army in coastal operations. Casualties to shipping and landing craft were not heavy, largely due to a very high degree of air superiority, an efficient anti-submarine organisation, and the achievement of tactical surprise.

Admiral Ramsay deplored the wide dispersal of planning authorities and the resulting prolonged period of negotiation, but was satisfied that the best available plan had been adopted, and that the weight of attack on a narrow front would overwhelm the enemy. The supporting fire from naval forces effectively dealt with the shelling from shore batteries. Also the moral effect of the rocket and gun landing craft firing from close inshore was considerable.

The immunity from air attack was surprising. Only three military transports and one hospital ship were lost in the anchorages in the first 3 days. From the naval point of view the first quarter of the moon may have been thought disadvantageous for landing operations. In the event, against a weak enemy, and with Allied air superiority, it proved advantageous, especially for the sailing of lightly escorted landing craft convoys.

Admiral Ramsay mentions that the question of the engagement of aircraft off the beaches was always a vexed one during planning. Orders were twice altered by agreement with the RAF. But he was firm that only in very exceptional circumstances should ships be deprived of their right to open fire at low-flying aircraft approaching them. The solution must be always to route transport aircraft clear of friendly shipping.

9 Supplementary Roles

He that Commands the sea is at great liberty, and may take as
much and as little of the war as he will.

BACON

Although the Allied navies had carried out the primary job of
putting the armies ashore, the task of landing reinforcements
and supplies had to continue without intermission. The battle
for the island was not yet won. The enemy was already bringing
in troops. The faster the advance of the Allied armies, the
swifter the flow of men and material, and the greater the need
for the maintenance and utilisation of sea and air power. The
principal objectives therefore of capturing airfields and ports
remained paramount and mutually beneficial. It is interesting
to recall that Mussolini, whose deposition was to come in just
2 weeks, continued to rely on the policy of a fleet in being. His
fleet of large and modern battleships would be safe in harbour.
Moreover, because of her central position in the Mediterranean,
Italy should be able to control the air in the seas around her
by shore-based aircraft. Long did he rue the day he had made
that decision and especially when Allied sea power was
enhanced by Britain's modern aircraft carriers providing
reconnaissance, and mobility of assault and defence. His battle
fleet would be highly vulnerable should it put to sea.

The Axis high command did its utmost to increase local air
power for the first few days after the Allied landings, and
thereby caused shipping losses, but there was not much that it
could do to counter Allied sea power while the Italian fleet

was kept in harbour. The port of Syracuse collapsed on D-day, giving Troubridge's Force A one of its main objectives after landing in ACID North. Early the next day, 11 July, the cruisers *Uganda* and *Mauritius* bombarded enemy positions as required. The approach channel was swept for mines, and a port party was put ashore to get Syracuse working. Mine-sweeping is a thankless task carried out in unknown waters abounding in hazards. Captain A. Patience writes:

> I was drafted to MMS 65. As we closed the enemy coast we could hear and see the gunfire, and our prayers were for those brave soldiers. However, we reached our allotted position in ACID North and continued to sweep all night and morning as the troops were still landing. They quickly moved inland, and the sound of gunfire got fainter. We encountered consistent air attacks, having a few near misses, as the main convoy of ships was about a mile south of us; and if the Eye-tie or Jerry had any bombs left we were always presented with the leavings.
>
> When Syracuse fell we were the first ship to be sent in, as we had to sweep the area for safety. On the way we saw the sickly sight of a stranded hospital ship [the *Aba*] that had been bombed.

Conditions in Syracuse at the time of surrender were deplorable. John Picken, a member of the naval beach signal section, writes:

> We were billeted on the top floor of what had been a government office in Syracuse. I have vivid recollections of the desperate hunger of the civil population who eagerly assailed the waste bins containing the left-overs of our own diet. Not having shaved for days, I visited a local barber, a swarthy Sicilian surrounded by his friends. As he produced his open razor it occurred to me that I was in a vulnerable situation, so I rather ostentatiously felt for my revolver, which was in its holster. However, everything passed off without incident and I was asked if I needed 'acqua', hair cream not being available.

Syracuse was not badly damaged, and by 13 July was able

Amphibious DUKW left centre of beach takes to the water (SCG)

to accept convoy MWS 37, which had anchored in the ACID area. Berthing and unloading were performed so efficiently that the ships were able to leave the same day. On the previous day, 12 July, Admiral Troubridge had embarked in the destroyer *Eskimo* at 4.30am with the intention of proceeding to the port of Augusta, 11 miles to the north of Syracuse; according to a signal made by Ramsay, it was being evacuated. The *Eskimo* was bombed and badly damaged, and Augusta was under enemy fire, so Troubridge transferred back to the *Bulolo*.

Augusta was certainly not being relinquished without a struggle, as can be gathered by the following letter from Commander R. A. Clarkson of the anti-aircraft cruiser *Carlisle*. After praising the gallant efforts of the young doctor of that ship in connection with the bombing and destruction of the *Talamba*, Clarkson says:

We in the *Carlisle* got into Syracuse on 12 July, taking with us the tail gunner of a Ju88. We had asked our Admiral [Troubridge] what to do with this prisoner and the reply was in

121

character. 'Give him to the army. This is supposed to be a combined operation.' In Syracuse harbour engineers were busily making hard standings to enable the LSTs to beach and discharge armour. I was told off by the First Lieutenant to take two marines and the motor dinghy and deliver our German prisoner to the army. This was more difficult than it looked, because the army were bent on getting out of the port area as soon as they could and did not want to hear about him. The prisoner himself, still carrying his parachute harness and deflated dinghy, clearly thought we were looking for a convenient place to shoot him. I eventually found a captain with a black beret in the main square; the German looked very relieved.

During that night's air raid an ammunition ship was hit in the harbour, which was covered with smoke. There was a gun accident in the next astern to us and our ship's company were dismayed by the screams of a badly wounded man.

The next day we left Syracuse and about mid-day pushed our bows tentatively into Augusta harbour. We were received by a fighter bomber which did no harm and I believe we were in

HMS Scarab *leads flotilla of landing craft for reloading* (SCG)

LST 365 beached at BARK south (JB)

fact the first major war vessel to enter the harbour. That night was hectic. The harbour was repeatedly attacked by three-engined SM79 Italian heavy bombers. At the same time Beau-fighters came out from Malta equipped with new radar. They decimated the enemy.

Unlike Syracuse, the port of Augusta put up quite a struggle. Entry was made twice on 12 July by a variety of smaller Allied ships and on each occasion accurate fire from ashore inflicted casualties and forced a withdrawal. Italian submarines were active offshore, and at 12.52pm the *Bonzo* happened to surface near the anti-submarine minesweeper *Seaham* which, together with other ships of the anti-submarine patrol, opened fire at close range. The *Seaham* sent a boarding party to capture the *Bonzo* (whose captain, together with five others, had been killed) and towed her into Syracuse. On the same day U409 was sunk by the British destroyer *Inconstant* off the Algerian coast after a 3-hour hunt, and U561 was torpedoed at close range by MTB 81 in the Straits of Messina. On the previous day, 11 July, the Italian submarine *Flutto* had been sunk by British MTBs off Catania.

At 7.30pm on 12 July, after dark, the *Ulster Monarch*, escorted by the destroyer *Tetcott* and two MGBs, entered Augusta harbour and landed a special raiding squadron. Opposition and heavy fire continued, and it was not until 13 July that the port capitulated. At 10.30am on that day the *Prins Albert* embarked No 3 Commando at Syracuse and proceeded to land them at 7.00pm at Punta Murazzo, 8 miles south of Catania. The *Tetcott* provided cover and later that night destroyed an enemy E-boat, one of three that were attacking the *Prins Albert*. Rear-Admiral Harcourt's cruisers were bombarding targets at Lentini, a strategic point 10 miles west-north-west of Augusta, still firmly held by the enemy; and were themselves being fired upon at extreme range that night. The monitor *Erebus* bombarded Catania, also at extreme range – 15 miles or more. The landing at Punta Murazzo was entirely successful, and paved the way for a northward advance along the east coast by 4 Armoured and 151 Infantry Brigades, thus by-passing Lentini for the time being.

Chief Gunner's Mate of LST 365 surveys Italian gun (JB)

The supporting gunfire and bombardment by Allied warships, provided as and when requested and exploiting Allied sea power, were proving most advantageous factors. Augusta was in Allied hands by 13 July, and within 24 hours enemy resistance there had ended. It was on the night of 13 July that the airborne landing to seize objectives near Catania had met misfortune, when troop-carrying aircraft passed over Allied shipping that shot many of them down in error. This may have seemed excusable in the case of those ships that found they were being bombed for longer and more frequent periods, owing to the bright moon. In addition, the fact that the enemy were switching air attacks from the American Western assault to the British Eastern assault meant that the distance to be covered by the Axis bombers was shorter. A smokescreen over the harbours and anchorages proved beneficial at night.

Two more Italian submarines were sunk on 13 July – the *Nereide* by the destroyers *Ilex* and *Echo*, and the *Acciaio* by the British submarine *Unruly*. Also on this day Rear-Admiral McGrigor relinquished his command of Force B to assume command and responsibility for the whole naval shore organisation in the Eastern assault area. His Force B duties were thereupon transferred to Rear-Admiral Vian. McGrigor's new title was Flag Officer, Sicily, and he was urgently required by Ramsay to proceed to Augusta to reorganise the administration of the Sicilian ports. Meanwhile Troubridge took charge of the port of Syracuse.

On 15 July General Montgomery's main Eighth Army headquarters were closed at Malta and transferred to Syracuse. This seemed a good omen; but already Axis opposition was increasing across the plains south of Catania, and the enemy's target for the main thrust was being shifted from the American Seventh Army front to the British Eighth Army. The decision had already been taken to land the British floating reserve, 78 Division, as Axis opposition grew, and for this reason beaches in the ACID area were earmarked and were to be maintained until such time as disembarkation could be completed.

LST 365 beaching near Cape Pachino (JB)

It is almost time to return to the Western assault to see what progress had been made since the successful landings of Patton's Seventh Army. But first a further word about the thorny problem of bombardment by supporting ships. Various difficulties were inherent in a feature which, certainly before the operation, was not universally accepted as feasible. The greatest stumbling block was the establishment of rapid communication and dependable understanding between the forward observation officer calling for support and the bombarding ship providing it. Careful regard had to be paid to the coding of exact requirements and the transmission of range and bearing.

On one occasion the monitor *Roberts* successfully carried out a bombardment of the undercliff road and railway at Taormina with her 15in guns. Air cover was provided, and spotting was done from two Spitfires belonging to Eighth Army Air Co-operation Squadron. Indirect fire opened at a range of 10 miles and, with the range closing, direct fire was employed as soon as the target became visible. A shore battery returned a heavy fire, but no hits were inflicted on the *Roberts*. The road and railway suffered direct hits. This form of bombardment with spotting aircraft was effectively used elsewhere, with salvoes up to 15 miles.

The headquarters ships used in Operation HUSKY were particularly suitable because of their comprehensive communications arrangements. Coordination between the three services in an amphibious operation depended as much on a rapid exchange of intelligence as it did on a will to cooperate. Reliable communication between advancing troops and headquarters was indispensable. The following short note shows one small side of the requirements. S. Hesketh writes:

> I served in the RAF, and my particular job was servicing radio and radar stations from a mobile workshop manned by three wireless mechanics, one of whom had to be able to drive. One of my first jobs was to salvage radio equipment from gliders which had landed in the sea somewhere south of Syracuse. We had no boats and had to swim out, and hold the equipment above our heads and swim back.
>
> Most of the radar vehicles were stationed in remote parts of the countryside and we travelled all over, servicing and repairing them. On first landing we were without tents and camped under trees.
>
> We travelled as far south as Noto and then made our way northwards up the east coast of Sicily.

The RAF had also organised servicing commandos. Squadron Leader Tweedie writes:

> Our duties were to refuel, rearm, and repair if necessary, guest aircraft arriving at an advanced landing ground before the main squadron arrived. If the situation turned sticky, the aircraft could return to their base and we could defend ourselves. Our transport was filled with mainly Spitfire spares.

Another indispensable feature was the photographic unit. B. A. Baker says:

> I was one of the RAF photographers who were landed just below Syracuse, our function being to process aerial

Local maps were primitive and scarce, so aerial photographs were vital for operations: mobile printing house and map centre

Map drawing under the lemon trees (CHWP)

photographs dropped from Malta-based aircraft by parachute, until such time as we could have our own airstrips laid down in Sicily. Amongst other vehicles, we landed two huge pantechnicon-type vehicles, quite enormous. Many of the troops thought them to be mobile houses of ill fame.

One hears little of the medical side of battles, although the non-combatants suffer many of the hazards and seem to get little thanks in return. Malaria was known to be one of the worst menaces ashore. Preparation had been made also for a large number of casualties from bomb, bullet, shell, and minefield. The following letter from an Army Nursing Sister, Miss Mary Luck, who was working in the hospital ship *Dorsetshire*, which followed the landing craft in the invasion, provides the woman's point of view and stresses the futility of war. The *Dorsetshire*, although fully illuminated (as was the *Talamba*) was bombed in the evening of 11 July and suffered damage and casualties. Miss Luck writes:

We dropped anchor and could see the men landing and taking a zig-zag path up the rising ground from the shore. We waited

129

Camouflage (CHWP)

all the afternoon, but no patients were brought on board until about 5.30pm, and these were not in great numbers. That night we lay at anchor, with guns firing over us, and without our lights on.

On the second evening we were told we could undress for the night, as we were going out of the anchorage, and would have the ship's lights on again.

About 5am I was awakened by a terrible noise and my tennis racket arriving on my head, and shrapnel or something flying across the cabin. I quickly donned my uniform overall and life jacket. I met the Chief Steward outside my cabin and between us we broke down the door on to the deck, as this was wedged, and I tripped down to my ward; I was met by the night orderly who said, 'He has gone, Sister, he died half an hour after you went off duty'. He referred to the man whose life we had been trying to save all day, and he thought this more important than the present happenings.

After our ship's engines were repaired, we sailed back to Alexandria with a full load of patients, then embarkation started again with patients to be taken home, as the Mediterranean was now open for ships to pass through the Straits of Gibraltar. As we were going through the Bay of Biscay – and the sea was choppy – it was whispered to us that we only had one lifeboat that was seaworthy; this was for 500 people, but we did not need it.

The men taken to Britain were the blind, the limbless, and the paralysed, people who would not be fit for war service again, yet they were so happy and excited to be going home. I often wondered how long they could keep up this front, when they had been separated from the mates they had shared experiences with, sent to specialised hospitals for their particular injuries, some to remain there for the rest of their lives, others to eventually go home and try to make a new life under difficult circumstances. Would the wives be able to cope with this change situation? Not even able to recognise their own husband in some cases. These are the ravages of war.

There were about sixty casualties when the Liberty Ship *Timothy Pickering*, unloading explosives in the ACID area, received a direct hit at noon on 13 July. A recent arrival, she blew up when hit, and covered the sea with blazing oil.

We have seen that close gunfire support for the troops landing during the assault on D-day was provided by bombardment groups comprising monitors and support craft, as well as by Force K under Rear-Admiral Harcourt in the *Newfoundland*. Once the initial phase was over, an inshore squadron was formed, on 13 July, under the orders of Flag Officer, Sicily, to

The transport Timothy Pickering *on fire* (SCG)

act in support of the army advancing northwards up the east
coast of Sicily. As the zone of military operations on the left
flank receded, so did the opportunities of bombardment in the
vicinity of the beaches. Nevertheless hardly a day passed
without ships being on call. Force K remained under the
operational control of the Commander-in-Chief, but was
available to Flag Officer, Sicily. Force K did excellent work,
but suffered damage and casualties when shelled, often at
long range, by unlocated batteries north of Catania.

The big ships of Force H and Force Z had performed the
manoeuvres designed to mislead the enemy. Greatly vulnerable
because of their size and only moderate speed, they were also
difficult to employ for long missions, owing to the limitations
of the destroyers with which it was essential to screen them.
By working watch and watch, however, one division could be

at sea while the second division was in harbour refuelling the destroyers. The battleships *Howe* and *King George V* of Force Z carried out a bombardment of Trapani on 12 July with the object of creating an impression that a descent was to be made on the west coast of Sicily, thus delaying any contemplated move of Axis troops to the British assault area in the south-east.

Not one warship was lost, other than LST 429 and subsidiary craft, but various ships of the bombardment groups were damaged. These included some destroyers, the cruisers *Cleopatra* and *Newfoundland*, and the monitors *Roberts* and *Erebus*. They had all distinguished themselves in their ardent support and prolific gunfire. No less distinguished were the actions of the motor torpedo boats, gunboats, motor launches, and the sweepers, who accounted for many of the enemy E-boats. Many were the battles at night in the Straits of Messina. In an audacious attack on the Italian cruiser *Regolo* before dawn, 17 July, MTB 316 was lost with all hands, and MTBs 260, 313, and 315 suffered damage and casualties, but the last that was seen of the *Regolo* was her dashing for Taranto at full speed.

In the very early hours of 16 July the carrier *Indomitable*, while in company with the 1st Division battleships *Nelson* and *Rodney*, the cruisers *Aurora* and *Penelope*, and a destroyer screen, was hit by a torpedo dropped from an enemy aircraft that flew right over this powerful assembly 50 miles eastwards of Cape Passero. The moon was full and the weather clear. Moreover *Indomitable* had six Albacores in the air maintaining an anti-surface-vessel search.

Flag Officer Force H, in his report, admitted that his division had been caught napping, and blamed this on the fact that there was almost a continuous presence of friendly aircraft, many of whom failed to establish their identity by means of IFF (Identification – Friend or Foe). Cunningham's comments on this inexcusable failure to shoot down the attacking aircraft ended by saying: 'An aircraft in a position to menace the fleet must be instantly engaged unless it has identified itself in the most positive manner.'

The *Indomitable*, at a reduced speed of 11 knots because of flooding, arrived at a rendezvous off Malta at 7.30am, where she was joined by 2nd Division of Force H and then entered the Grand Harbour. The carrier *Formidable* parted company with 2nd Division to join 1st Division, which then proceeded to sea to cover the north-eastern approaches. Meanwhile an urgent call was received by Cunningham for a heavy bombardment of Catania on 17 July. The *Valiant* had fouled her port propeller and was temporarily unavailable. The *Warspite* thereupon proceeded with the *Euryalus* and a large destroyer escort to Catania, where at speed and with ranges not less than 6 miles she fired fifty-five 15in shells. To reach the bombarding position the *Warspite* made good $23\frac{1}{2}$ knots, which was remarkably fast for a battleship almost thirty years of age. Cunningham made a signal to his former flagship, a veteran of battles off Calabria, Matapan, and Crete: 'Operation well carried out. There is no doubt that when the old lady lifts her skirts she can run.' The Eighth Army appreciated those bombardments, which were laid on at specific times and places at their request. They remarked that they were accurate and timely.

The operation to capture Sicily was still very far from won, and already a stubborn resistance was stiffening. Command of the sea and the air had been indispensable. If the enemy should resolutely dig in on the plains of Catania, and the Gerbini airfields remain in their hands, both of which events seemed likely, there was still the opportunity for 'he that commands the sea' to use the sea and put heavy forces ashore behind the enemy front, or at any chosen point. One of the biggest obstacles was Mount Etna and its indifferent paths, but perhaps that could be by-passed too.

10 The Struggle for Sicily

After the difficult landings experienced by the Americans on the south-west coast, and the initial armoured opposition they faced at Gela, Patton's Seventh Army had shown great spirit and had advanced rapidly to the north-west, protecting the left flank of 1 Canadian Division. Meanwhile, as planned by Montgomery, his own Eighth Army had pushed on northwards through Syracuse and Augusta, rapidly at first, but more slowly as it met growing German resistance on the plains of Catania and its approaches (see Maps 3 and 4). Strategic features in the advance to Catania were two bridges, about 7 miles apart. One was the Malati bridge across the Lentini River, and the other was the Primosole bridge across the River Simeto. It was necessary to take both in order to capture the airfields at Gerbini and Catania. The fighting that developed in this vicinity was probably as savage as any in the whole operation.

As early as 11 July Colonel Schmalz of the Hermann Goering Division had pushed his Schmalz battle-group southward on the Catania plains, and had been reinforced the following day when 1 German Parachute Division began to arrive at the Catania airfields.

The objective of British XIII Corps had been to make a bridgehead across the Simeto River by 14 July and then to capture Catania. For this purpose 5 Division and 50 Division were to press northwards on roughly parallel tracks along the eastern littoral. Ahead of these two advancing divisions, the Malati bridge across the Lentini River was to be seized by

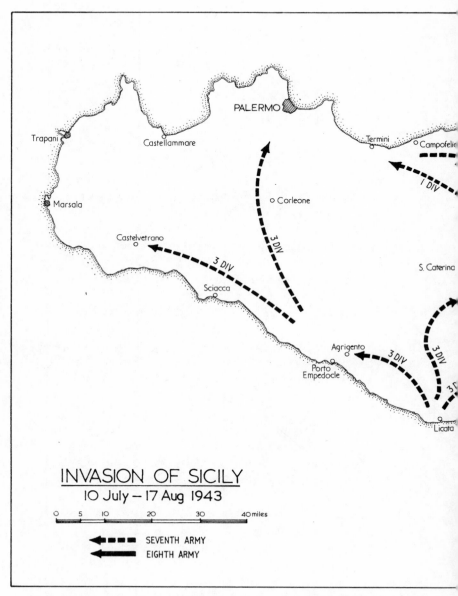

PALERMO

Trapani

Castellammare

Termini

Campofelic

1 DIV

Marsala

Corleone

3 DIV

Castelvetrano

3 DIV

S. Caterina

Sciacca

3 DIV

Agrigento

3 DIV

3 DIV

3 DIV

3 F

Porto
Empedocle

Licata

INVASION OF SICILY
10 July – 17 Aug 1943

0   5   10   20   30   40 miles

SEVENTH ARMY
EIGHTH ARMY

Map 4   Invasion of Sicily: rough routes of Allied ground forces

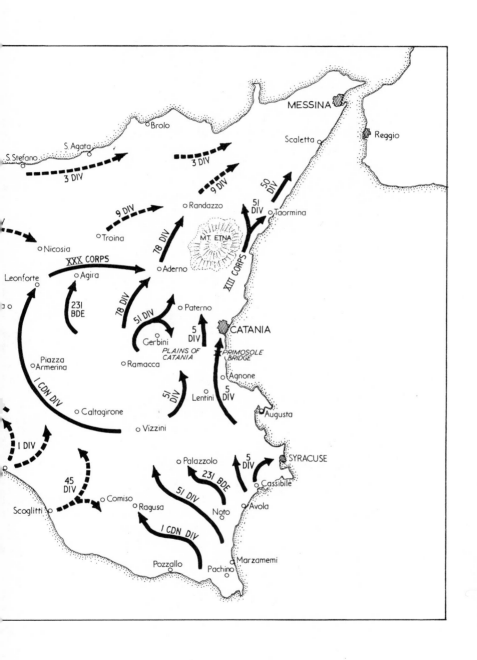

3 Commando, landing from the sea in the vicinity of Agnone, supported as necessary by gunfire from ships. The bridge was about 5 miles inland from Agnone and its capture had been timed to take place a few hours before the expected arrival of 5 and 50 Divisions. Schmalz with his elusive battle-group managed to delay and frustrate their hopes.

As we have seen, 3 Commando landed successfully from the *Prins Albert* near Agnone at 10.30pm on 13 July and captured Malati bridge at 4.00am the next morning. There was, however, no sign of the expected British force from Lentini, and to avoid possible heavy casualties to the group of 400 men, it was decided to withdraw. Charges on the bridge had been skilfully removed, so the landing did succeed in leaving the bridge intact for later use by XIII Corps.

The airborne venture for Primosole bridge (see Chapter 7) was tragically chaotic because of gunfire from Allied ships. Fourteen aircraft were lost, and twenty-six returned to Africa without dropping their loads. But by 6.30am, 14 July, about 120 British troops had fought their way to the bridge and removed demolition charges, and were guarding their prize with three anti-tank guns. HMS *Newfoundland* gave valuable help in the matter of supporting gunfire. By the time the relieving force of 4 and 151 Brigades arrived on the scene there had been some tough fighting, with what Montgomery's Chief of Staff described as fanatical savagery.

In 151 Brigade was Tony Pridham, a platoon commander with 8 Battalion Durham Light Infantry, who writes:

I landed near Avolo on D-day. I lasted only until the crossing of the Simeto River and the Primosole bridge battle and was probably the first member of the Eighth Army to cross the bridge. I was later the only one to live of four who returned to the bridge in the carrier which was knocked out just on the south side of the bridge. I made contact with a tank lying near a wrecked glider just south of the bridge.

Another participant was Major-General Martin, who was at that time a company commander supporting 151 Infantry Brigade. Having referred to the extraordinary sensation of travelling to war in a luxury liner, and the incongruity of being called to breakfast by Indonesian waiters tinkling gongs, before swarming down the nets to the assault landing craft, he speaks of the contrast of such luxuries when measured against the 'ugly fighting round the Primosole bridge'.

One who took part in the unfortunate airborne attack on Primosole bridge was Major G. H. Seal, who at that time was signal sergeant of 21 Independent Parachute Company. Seal says:

The operation was suspended for some reason for 24 hours. But on the beautiful clear evening of Friday 13 July we reassembled. The CO 1 Parachute Battalion (Alistair Pearson, who later became Brigade Commander and won four DSOs) was wearing no badges of rank, a plain khaki shirt and dirty plimsolls. We knew that the job was on.

At about 8.30pm we took off from Tunisia and had a quiet flight, though it seemed much longer than a direct route would have taken. Light flak was fairly regular. I remember reflecting briefly that it wasn't a bad firework display. Our American pilot was flying very low; in fact, standing in the doorway, I was disconcerted that I was able, in the gloom, to discern quite easily the individual branches of the olive trees. The terrain was dissimilar to that one expected around the dropping zone.

As the green light came on, I went out like a bomb. My parachute opened and I hit the ground immediately on a hillside. My corporal was nearby. We never saw anything of the others in our stick.

All around us every activity, German and Italian, was intense. If any pattern revealed itself it was probably that the former seemed to be heading north, and the Italians south. My corporal not wishing to proceed, I set off walking into the darkness. It was clear that the dropping zone was not in this neighbourhood. Accordingly I destroyed my pathfinding equipment by explosive. My course was north-east, but I had many stops, always to hide.

139

Battle-torn observation post near Primosole (DLCP)

The operational objective for 1 Parachute Brigade was the capture of Primosole bridge, and the holding of it for 48 hours. The bridge is the entrance to the plain of Catania, and the Brigade task was to facilitate the passage of Eighth Army. Brigadier Gerald Lathbury, with a tiny force, captured the bridge and held it for many hours. I believe he performed excellently on a Bren gun. I never found the bridge.

At first light I identified a north facing strip of the east coast and realised that the bridge was several miles to the north of my position. An Italian commando captain, with his sixty or so armed men, came up and pleaded with me to take them all prisoner. I asked him to get lost, which he did.

Seeing what I thought to be a German patrol, I ran into a pillbox and found an undamaged Italian machine gun, and trained the gun on the group. The group soon revealed itself as a British airborne collection. We occupied an adjacent farmyard and took up defensive positions. Soldiers filtered in and gradually our numbers built up. We assumed the bridge had been won or lost for we were ordered to make south, away from the scene, to Syracuse.

The first advancing Eighth Army vehicle was driven by a sergeant whose passenger was General Montgomery. He asked me some very pertinent questions and was given some straightforward comments on aircraft navigation. He spoke in a quiet and friendly way, gave me a cigarette and passed slowly on.

The whole affair had been thoroughly disappointing. If it had not been postponed, and with better navigation, the operation could have been a brilliant success.

We have seen three aspects by men who were at Primosole in different categories. Here is a further one, giving the Royal Artillery point of view. Captain D. L. C. Price, RA, writes:

I was one of the advance party of 124 Field Regiment in 50 Division. We soon got ashore with our armoured carrier, and our first act was to cook breakfast. Happily there was little local resistance, but I was conscious that the Army was not fully alive to the absolute necessity to move inland quickly, for our toehold would not save us in the event of a counterattack.

One sunny afternoon I went on a reconnaissance with Major Paul Parberry, OC 288 Battery, and was disturbed to hear a loud explosion in front; his half track vehicle had gone over a land mine and I think all the occupants were killed.

The battle by now was taking shape and I remember shelling Carlentini, a suburb of Lentini, and then an hour later using up all our dressings bandaging up the civilian wounded after entering the town. They were very understanding and all the church bells were ringing, so I didn't feel too badly, and in any case nobody was seriously hurt. But the futility of war was again brought to my mind by that incident.

The battle became really serious at the Simeto river, the south boundary of the Catania plain, because a German Panzer Division had joined the fray. For the next 10 days the fighting there was the bitterest I remember in the whole war and I can still smell the stench of decaying flesh on the banks of that river. Eventually, the Durham Light Infantry Brigade under Ronnie Senior, in a brilliant operation, got over the river to the other side. During those 10 days I had an observation post in a smart villa overlooking the plain, which had a convenient turret but which seemed to offer target practice for the German anti-tank gunners, who used to put the odd shell through it, but fortunately lower down! I had several visitors. One was a smartly dressed Lieut RN who said he had 'a monitor' and could he help. I apologised for my ignorance and he explained it was a seaborne 15in gun. I asked him his accuracy of ranging and he said 'about a hundred yards'. I declined his help!

The night came to press across the Catania plain, and those were a few bad hours. More than a few soldiers 'turned and ran'. We had the luggage carrier on our vehicle carried away by an anti-tank shell while we were in it! I did an on-foot reconnaissance and we 'holed-up' behind a haystack until dawn; which heralded a better day. We pressed across the plain but the Quartermaster's department of the infantry hadn't caught up and, by the evening, the PBI (poor bloody infantry) had had no food. This fact, unknown of course to them, did not deter a German machine-gun crew from firing into the positions selected for a night's rest and sustenance. The Company Commander 'lent' me ten volunteers and, as the sun was setting, we went out, up a vine-covered hill, hoping to finish the day successfully. It was not entirely to be. We had to withdraw but left nobody behind. The gesture persuaded the Germans to go; so there was rest after all. We always carried our own rations and cooking equipment. There was a hen for eggs in the tool box and a hot

Top storey of villa overlooking Simeto river (DLCP)

water pan on the exhaust manifold for cooking tins of stew. I remember extensive use of mines about this phase of the affair and sitting on the bonnet of the tracked carrier looking for a disturbed surface on paths we followed, touching the driver's shoulder to stop when suspicion arose. There was no time for 'sweeping' ahead; we had to get on. One less lucky carrier had been blown up into a tree and was lodged forlornly in a leafy grave.

After the Catania plain had been taken on 5 August, I think the Germans knew that they were going to lose and we made better progress. The next event was Taormina and the order went out to take it without damage. We took a chance and drove up the hill into the town at dawn, 15 August, and the risk paid off – there were no enemy. We breakfasted in the square and the Mayor came and offered us the keys of the town and two bottles of champagne. The keys I returned and he shared the champagne with us; it was a very friendly little

Bridge across Simeto, scene of bloodiest fighting (DLCP)

ceremony and gradually the people came out to look, to chatter, and to embrace.

As the day advanced, the infantry caught up and so did my guns and we went into action on the plateau of the promontory above the beautiful Isola Bella bay. It was here that Air Vice-Marshal Broadhurst nearly didn't live to fight another day as he put down his little plane in front of the guns just as we were opening fire. Happily, I saw the aeroplane coming in and shouted 'stop' which gunners know means just that.

The rest of the day was somehow sad. The road had been blown and we had to put our gear on our backs and walk. As the Germans retreated, so they blew up a vital road bridge on that east coast shore line and we were able to pursue them no more.

The Axis commanders had not been slow in realising the strategic advantages of their defensive position on the plains of Catania and wasted no time before establishing a barrier, a metaphorical gate between Catania on the east coast and S.

Stefano on the north coast. The hingepost stood at Catania. The gate would close about this hinge, and so shut out the Allies. It would provide a stopper for the Americans in the west who were capturing and consolidating key points while protecting the left flank of the Canadians; and would act as an effective obstacle to the 50 and 51 British Divisions, which were now moving northwards on parallel routes tending to converge as they approached the plains of Catania (see Map 4). Twenty miles north of Catania was another barrier, Mount Etna, strategically of the utmost value to the Axis defence. East of Etna was a single coastal road leading northwards, vulnerable to sabotage, and hence a further defensive advantage to retreating Axis troops. The British failure and forced delay in breaking out northwards of the Simeto river allowed the Axis to bring in further reinforcements, including German paratroops, and to occupy strong positions along the southern and western foothills of Mount Etna.

By 16 July the Primosole bridge had been recaptured by the British after some very fierce fighting, and a bridgehead had been established. Catania seemed to be within reach, being then only 5 miles to the north. A frontal attack on the city was launched in the early hours of 18 July. Two brigades of Kirkman's 50 Division met fierce opposition and suffered heavy losses without gaining ground. Montgomery wished to broaden his front. On 20 July he ordered the reserve 78 Division to be brought from Sousse in Tunisia, but they were held up by lack of transport after landing, and took, in some cases, more than a week to reach the front. About 500 vehicles had been lost on 4 July when the *City of Venice* and the *St Essylt* were torpedoed off the African coast.

It was thereupon decided that to persist in the frontal attack on Catania would result in casualties too heavy to be acceptable. Instead there was to be a three-pronged flanking attack in the shape of a triple left hook. I have two letters from participants who took part in this crucial manoeuvre, and both are worth recording, as they illustrate so well the apparent deadlock that suddenly seemed to have arisen because of Montgomery's serious setbacks. The first letter is from H. I. Tait, a twenty-year-old soldier of 51 Highland Division.

Our battalion was to attack and capture the Gerbini airfield on the night of 20 July. The plan was to attack along the line of a railway and capture the main road and clear it for transport. Since this was a night attack, the line of advance was on compass bearings and the distance covered had to be carefully timed in order to keep up with a rolling artillery barrage. The start line was a deep ditch running at right-angles to the railway, this ditch being at least 15ft deep with thick barbed wire on the enemy side. This obstacle delayed the start of the advance and it was not long before we knew that we were up against strong enemy opposition as enemy machine-gun fire was very accurate, and we incurred heavy casualties during the first half mile of the advance. After fierce fighting we eventually found ourselves on the airfield perimeter but were pinned down by accurate and deadly fire from enemy pillboxes, and the tanks which were supporting us seemed unable to relieve the situation. There were several counterattacks by German troops which were identified as units from the Hermann Goering Division and Paratroops. At about 9.00am, 21 July, there was a counterattack by German tanks supported by about a battalion strength of infantry. In the confused fighting which developed I was captured by a section of Paratroops. Fortunately they did not search me very thoroughly and failed to see a Biretta automatic pistol I had in a shoulder holster partially hidden by the straps on my equipment. I was sent back with one young soldier as an escort – he was a voluble Bavarian and whether he was distracted by our conversation I am not sure, but he made the mistake of walking in front of me, and when we were going through some trees I got out my revolver, pressed it in his neck, relieved him of his machine pistol and told him to run for his life. He quickly disappeared northward; I travelled southward even more quickly.

During the fighting before daylight I had been wounded twice (in the arm and side); consequently, when I managed to make my way back to our unit, I was evacuated. Our battalion losses had been severe, so I was able to return to the unit within about 10 days, although neither of the wounds had healed.

146

One point I had particularly noted during the battle was the vulnerability of the Sherman tank, which had a much higher outline than the German tanks, and seemed to be picked off very easily. Our CO was killed whilst in a tank conferring with the tank commander. It was probably early August before our battalion went back into action. I recollect that one of our infantry companies captured a self-propelled 75mm gun by dropping into it from a tree as the gun proceeded along the road. This gun we retained.

The second letter is from Lieut Michael Aldworth, a platoon commander of 7 Battalion Royal Marines, which on 19 July was placed under the command of 51 Highland Division. Reference to Maps 1 and 4 will prove helpful. Aldworth writes:

The Battalion suddenly received orders to reform as an infantry battalion. What had happened was that Eighth Army had met increasing resistance on the Catania Plain as the German divisions deployed into defensive positions and the Army Commander with only four infantry divisions (5, 50, 51, and 1 Canadian) plus the later-landed 78 was looking round for any spare infantry he could find. I assume that Montgomery included marines in the classification of infantry, though my impression is that he never had much time for the Corps.

Accordingly, with transport for only one company, the remainder having to march, we moved the 60 or 70 miles northwards through Noto, Palazzolo, Buccheri, Vizzini, Caltagirone, thence by a roundabout route to Ramacca, all this taking two or three days. My company, Y, formed the advance-guard and had most of the benefit of the transport, though a system of ferrying was used.

My three-ton lorry, which with its lance-corporal RASC driver had been up and down the desert for years, broke down in the centre of Ramacca; my Company Commander stopped for a moment, told me that the rendezvous was a junction of five tracks just to the south-east of Mount S. Giovanni, which he indicated with his finger, and said that our task was to advance across the Dittaino River, clearing Catenanuova and digging in on the far side. With that, he and the rest of the unit disappeared in a cloud of dust.

147

After some time the lorry was persuaded to start again, and with a map I made my way with the major part of my platoon by the most direct route to the rendezvous, little knowing that the battalion had moved by a much more circuitous route with the result that when I reached the tracks junction, there was no sign of anyone, though guns were firing on the right front as 51 Division probed towards the Gerbini airfield complex. I decided that the battalion had already moved on up the track and was just about to proceed in the same direction in the lorry when I spotted the Mortar officer running towards me waving his arms. I stopped the driver and soon learned that the battalion hadn't yet arrived and that if I went up the track, I would be blown off the face of the earth by a battery of 88s as soon as I got over the brow of the hill.

I naturally de-bussed and awaited the arrival of the battalion. (This was the afternoon of 19 July.) Later, two fellow Y company officers and myself went up the track by foot to make a reconnaissance and it was then that we saw that the enemy's defensive line was not merely held by Italian troops, as had been thought, but had formations of Germans there as well, later identified as the Hermann Goering Division. However, nobody believed us and preparations were made for a night attack, which we afterwards spoke of as the battle of Massiera Parlato.

The action was an utter failure for us, though there is no doubt that the junior leaders and marines of A and B Companies displayed tons of guts, they being the assaulting companies. When daylight came, everybody was pinned down by MG, shell, mortar, and rifle fire. Inevitably we had to withdraw to the foothills on our side of the river. Poor intelligence, indifferent planning, and almost complete lack of supporting arms (two 3.7 howitzers, which were soon knocked out) were the reasons. The whole of the Army seems to have suffered in the same way.

We spent the next week in the line in the same position and then moved round to the Gerbini sector for another week, during which the Contra Fico d'India feature was taken by a four-battalion Brigade of the Highland Division; Agira and Regalbuto by 231 Brigade and the Canadians; and night explosions in the Gerbini area indicated that the enemy was preparing for withdrawal. This indeed was the case and one morning we had the satisfaction of watching British tanks cross the river and railway at Sferro [five miles north-west of Gerbini], bring to action a group of German tanks and force their withdrawal.

The fortnight or so in the line, starting with the action at Massiera Parlato, had been a sobering experience, and we had lost a good many men, particularly on 20 July. The weather was extremely hot, and water severely rationed so that life was anything but comfortable by day and of course made busy by patrols etc: by night. In addition, many of us had picked up the malaria bug, and although this was kept under by the regular dose of mepachrine at the time, it came out in a lot of cases including my own the following year in NW Europe.

I recall one amusing incident during this period. One morning, several of my platoon asked my permission to climb the hill in rear of our position to a cattle water trough for a bath (and no doubt a drink, as we were very parched!). I reminded them that the trough was under enemy observation, but they thought that if they were careful, they would not be spotted. There was no reason otherwise why they shouldn't go, so I said 'yes' and off they went. Our dress at this time was khaki shorts and shirts, our faces, hands and knees being tanned dark brown by the sun. All went well until they took their shirts and shorts off, when the white parts of their bodies attracted the attention of the opposition gunners and very soon there arrived the first of a number of murderous salvoes from the 88s on the other side of the river. My men picked up their clothes and ran as fast as they could go, down the hill stark naked closely followed by shellbursts, eventually reaching our position safely without casualty. The rest of us laughed our heads off!

When the Catania Plain front collapsed, 5 August, our battalion was brought round to the seaward end of the Plain where the main road from Lentini to Catania approaches the latter city past the airport. There, we were told that 50 Division had by-passed Catania to chase the opposition to Messina and that we were to enter and clear Catania of enemy troops. Y Company led the advance and 16 Platoon was the 'point' platoon of the whole show! I had visions of desperate street fighting with 'do or die' Hermann Goering troops making last stands at every street corner. Fortunately, they had had enough and were being pulled back to the Italian mainland. Accordingly, we marched into Catania, the first formed body of troops there, and were greeted by polite hand-claps from the population, who seemed glad that we had arrived!

Meanwhile as the battle developed there had been many changes in Alexander's Army Group plan, which are worth following in a little detail. By the end of D+1 he was optimistic. Both Seventh and Eighth Armies were safely ashore, and nearly everywhere were pushing ahead as though nothing could stop them. At that time he was particularly anxious to deny the enemy the main east-west routes in the centre of Sicily; the further north Alexander's armies could penetrate beyond the central area, the more difficult would the enemy find a withdrawal to Messina if they decided to evacuate.

The task for Eighth Army was for XIII Corps to push northwards, capturing the ports of Augusta and Catania, and the Gerbini group of airfields on the eastern coast. At the same time XXX Corps was to push northwards to the centre, broadening the front. (Map 4 shows very simply the routes of the various Allied groups. The tracks make no claim for accuracy or completeness, and are intended as a complement to the narrative. For fuller information concerning towns and main roads, see Map 1.) Seventh Army was to be free to pivot on its left, but its main task must be to establish itself on the left flank of Eighth Army. This was the gist of Alexander's instructions to both armies late on 13 July, by which date the opposition in the Augusta-Catania region was stiffening rapidly, as has been described. General Patton was surprised and disappointed with these instructions, which seemed to give Seventh Army a subsidiary holding role in west-central Sicily, depriving them of an opportunity for offensive action, and allowing Eighth Army to become the main striking force.

On 13 July Kesselring appointed General Hube as Corps commander in Sicily. This was less than 2 weeks before Mussolini's downfall on 25 July. Hitler was concerned that the Italians might withdraw from the Axis, in which case he would wish to evacuate German troops through the gateway to Messina as securely as possible and with a shortening rearguard as they approached Messina at the apex of a triangle. Hube was to take tactical control. In the meantime German

150

reinforcements were being sent to Sicily in the shape of units of 1 Parachute Division, and 29 Panzer Grenadier Division to add to 15 Panzer Grenadiers and the Hermann Goering Division. The 29 Panzers were in the northern sector of his defences, the 15 Panzers in the centre, and the Hermann Goering in the east. The remnants of three Italian divisions also fought with the Germans.

On 16 July, the day that the Primosole bridge had been recaptured, Alexander issued a directive to Montgomery and Patton. Eighth Army, after capturing Catania and the Gerbini airfields, would drive the enemy into the Messina triangle along three main lines:

1 Northward along the coastal road from Catania, leaving Mount Etna on the left;
2 Eastward from Leonforte, then northward round the west side of Mount Etna to complete a pincers movement;
3 Eastward from Nicosia along Highway 120, leading in the direction of Messina via Randazzo.

With the benefit of hindsight it seems obvious that such tactics would tend to drive the enemy towards withdrawal from Messina rather than confine him in a bag leading to surrender. In fact Catania would not be captured until 5 August and the Gerbini airfields were to hold out with stubborn German defence until 21 July, despite the heavy thrust and attempts to break through by Eighth Army at great cost.

But Alexander's instructions had a sting in the tail for Patton. He had earlier been warned to leave Highway 124 clear for Montgomery's left flank in the general movement north-west. But now Seventh Army was to protect the rear of Eighth Army as it proceeded northward! Patton felt that Seventh Army had been assigned a passive mission. He made his case to Alexander, who issued a fresh directive on 18 July which would permit him to push northwards and westwards to 'mop up the western half of Sicily'. Alexander seems to have been unaware of the resentment his directives caused, since as Army Group Commander he was singularly dedicated to the proper coordination and understanding between his two armies, and the reconciliation of the very different points of view held by his two Army commanders. His earlier decisions had practically shaped the issue, but they ignored two points: first that Catania was to become a virtual stalemate, with the Germans in an almost unassailable position on the plains south of Etna; and second the tremendous drive and enterprise of Patton.

It is interesting to speculate about probable events had Alexander's earlier directives allocated his two armies reverse roles. It is feasible that if 45 US Division had not been warned off Highway 124 they would instead have reached the important central network of roads some days earlier than 1 Canadian Division reached it in isolation. With it, 51 Highland Division, 1 Canadian Division, and 231 Malta Brigade, XXX Corps would then have remained concentrated, advancing northwards to Paterno (12 miles west of Catania). The battle for Paterno, fought by 51 Division on the defensive on 21 July, would accordingly have been fought by the whole Corps. Paterno would have fallen before the end of July and with it the defences in the Catania plain. It is perhaps a rather pointless argument, however, with too many ifs and buts.

As it was, Montgomery realised by 21 July that the enemy was going to hold Catania to the last, and he must shift the main weight of his Eighth Army offensive to the left flank, where 1 Canadian Division were doing so well, having captured Leonforte that day. He would also reinforce that flank with 78 Division, which on 20 July he had ordered to be brought over from Sousse and which was now becoming available for the front. On the right of the Canadians 231 Brigade had also been doing well, but was stopped at Agira by a vigorous counter-offensive that was to last until 28 July.

Meanwhile there was no holding Patton, whose army overran the entire western half of Sicily in the last 10 days of

July. The 3 US Division, after landing at Licata under Truscott, had quickly proceeded north-westwards along the coast to Agrigento and Porto Empedocle. They entered Corleone on 21 July and moved on to accept the surrender of Palermo the following day. The 45 US Division, which had landed at Scoglitti under Middleton, also pushed on quickly to Termini via S. Caterina, and then turned east for Campofelice. At San Stefano 45 Division were relieved by 3 Division, which passed through them prior to their leapfrog along the coastal road to Saint Agata, 8 August, mentioned below. The 1 US Division, in accordance with Alexander's new plan, received orders from Patton to push eastwards with maximum pressure via Petralia and Nicosia towards Randazzo along Highway 120. This thrust was to be combined with the supporting advance along the north coastal road Highway 113. Allied air attacks were now concentrating on the German armour, in particular 15 Panzer Grenadiers. The latter withdrew to a strongly defensive north-south line which ran through Regalbuto conforming roughly with 29 Panzer Grenadiers to the north of them and the Hermann Goering Division to the south, all prepared for a bloody struggle to the death.

Owing to the static defensive position adopted by the Germans, with the ever-open door available to Messina, if and when required, the majority of troops (Allied and German) were now very roughly becoming confined within a shrinking area of less than 25 miles square. Naval gunfire support for the various actions inland was therefore out of the question, except for the US division advancing along the north coastal road, which was strongly supported by US ships. That division was suffering considerable casualties and delays from demolitions and mining inflicted by the retiring enemy. Patton, as usual full of enterprise, called for an amphibious leapfrog operation whereby Task Group 88 based on Palermo under Rear-Admiral Davidson, USN, composed of landing ships and landing craft with cruisers and destroyers in support, were to by-pass the enemy at a particularly tough spot near San

Stefano, where the Germans had intended a prolonged stand. The embarkation took place on 7 August and the troops were disembarked further east at S. Agata, without loss, on 8 August. The leapfrog, however, accomplished little, as the Germans, anxious about their own evacuation, had already begun to withdraw eastward at speed. Cunningham made a signal to Davidson to the effect that two Italian light cruisers, the *Garibaldi* and the *Duca d'Aosta*, were on the prowl, and hopes ran high that Davidson's covering ships would intercept. The Italians, however, ran into fog and deemed it wiser to retire. The appointments of Admirals Ramsay and Hewitt had come to an end, 19 July, and thereafter the support and supply of troops in Sicily became a routine operation under Cunningham as C-in-C Mediterranean.

Morison is of the opinion that this amphibious landing at S. Agata gained very little, owing to the timing. A week earlier and the Germans would have been squeezed out of Troina and Regalbuto. As it was, 1 US Division on Highway 120 had to fight a considerable battle for Troina in the first week of August, as did 1 Canadian Division for Regalbuto. Hindsight makes it all so obvious. What is certain is that 15 Panzer Grenadiers and the remnants of the Italian Aosta Division put up tremendous counterattacks, being eventually overcome by superior Allied artillery and air power. It is clear that sea power supported by air power was indispensable to the Allies: the reserve 78 British Division had been disembarked at Syracuse 25–8 July, and the US Seventh Army 9 Division reserve had landed at Palermo on 1 August. The newly arrived 78 Division captured Centuripe on 2 August and entered the key town of Aderno on 7 August. The Americans conducted two more leapfrogs along the north coast after their S. Agata landing, but by then the Germans were on the move eastwards at such a pace that interception was difficult. After the fierce battle for Troina, 1 US Division were relieved by the reserve 9 Division, which passed through them and pushed east to capture Cesaro on 8 August, before pressing on for Randazzo.

Cunningham was full of praise for Patton's enterprise and the manner in which the subsidiary amphibious operations were conducted with such skill and energy. He deplores the fact that the Eighth Army failed to take a leaf out of the American book and use the sea to get behind the enemy lines, especially during the stalemate at Catania. He writes: 'We had the ships ready at Augusta with commando troops embarked for just such operations, and I was sure that with Rear-Admiral McGrigor, full of fire and energy, in charge, operations of this sort would have been no less successful than those on the north coast.'

One successful landing did take place on the east coast on the night of 15 August at Scaletta, 8 miles south of Messina, by 40 RM Commando with tanks, guns, and vehicles. Montgomery understandably appears to have lacked enthusiasm for such an operation, despite the fact that supporting ships were in attendance. 'The enemy had already withdrawn north of the area,' he says, 'and owing to demolitions on the Corniche road the force was unable to advance either to the north or south. A party moved inland on foot, seeking a route across country to Messina.'

The monitor *Roberts*, aided by aircraft spotting, engaged a battery that was firing from the shore at a range of 15 miles and silenced it with her 15in guns.

Montgomery flew to visit Patton in his newly established headquarters in Palermo on 28 July, and tactics for a big offensive were discussed. With the two armies converging on the restricted area held by the enemy it was important that questions concerning boundaries and roads should be settled. Convinced that the enemy would hold on to Catania until the last possible moment, and that a direct advance on that axis would result in very heavy casualties, Montgomery decided that it would be more effectual to make a thrust towards Aderno with XXX Corps enlarged by the addition of 78 Division. An offensive to the north would proceed via Centuripe, Aderno, and Randazzo, and the target date for a full-scale drive on the enemy was to be 1 August, three long eventful weeks after those successful landings on the beaches, since when the Allied troops had become battle-hardened but tired.

On the left of Eighth Army the American Seventh Army, as we have seen, had been grouped by Patton to develop two separate divisional thrusts eastward, one along coast road 113, the other from Nicosia through Troina along road 120 to Randazzo. On the right of the Americans and some 20 miles south of them was 1 Canadian Division moving eastwards along road 121 through Leonforte (which they had captured on 21 July), and Agira (28 July) and onwards to Regalbuto and Aderno. This was to be supported in a northerly thrust by 78 Division along the Aderno-Bronte axis. Two divisions, 51 Highland and 5 Division, were to remain on the defensive, maintaining aggressive raids in order to pin the opposing enemy formations in their existing positions.

The newly arrived 78 Division under Major-General Evelegh showed great form in capturing Centuripe on 3 August from a very determined enemy. With this stronghold in Allied hands, and the capture of Regalbuto by 1 Canadian Division and 231 Brigade, the possession of the key town of Aderno became a certainty. Montgomery refers to a most interesting capture of a map of enemy dispositions clearly showing Aderno as the key to the German Etna position.

The enemy were now systematically on the move. But it was a slow retirement with a strong rearguard action. It was even slower for the Allied armies on a narrowing front, for they not only had to fight fiercely for every town but had to face booby traps, mines, and demolitions along the limited and damaged roads.

Catania fell at last on 5 August, as did Misterbianco and Paterno. On 6 August 9 US Division, lately brought in as a reserve, captured Troina after a long and bloody battle, and 51 Highland Division took Biancavilla near Aderno. On 7 August 78 Division took Aderno after very heavy fighting and a sudden withdrawal by the enemy.

A vast armada (IWM)

With the fall of Aderno the main defence line across north-eastern Sicily was broken, and the enemy was retreating on all sectors. Aerial reconnaissance revealed increasing traffic across the Straits of Messina. The retreating German troops now reaped the benefit of the shape of the land, for as the Allied forces were all the time converging, so they became inevitably slower and more easily delayed.

The 3 US Division had been progressing rapidly along the north coast, closely supported by the cruiser *Philadelphia*, Davidson's flagship, and destroyers. Twice they carried out amphibious operations between S. Agata and Brolo, as previously executed by part of 45 US Division at S. Stefano. The idea was to cut off the retreating enemy and to accelerate their own speed of advance but, as related before, it proved in-effectual, owing to the great pace of enemy withdrawal. The 9 US Division captured Randazzo on 13 August at the same time as 78 Division were fighting strongly to the south of this crossroads town. The 5 Division had been relieved by 51 Highland Division which, having taken the easterly route round Etna, captured Linguaglossa on 15 August. The 50 Division, even further east along the east coast road, and advancing northward, occupied Taormina the same day. The end was in sight.

Surgeon Captain V. Gartside relates an incident about Taormina that is worth recounting. It concerns the small gunboat HMS *Cockchafer*, which was patrolling off Taormina just before the surrender of that town. She sailed close inshore and fired a number of salvoes into Taormina. After the first few shots, white flags rapidly appeared amongst the houses as a token of surrender. The prisoners then made their way eagerly to the beach. A Maltese steward on board the gunboat shouted at the prisoners in Italian, and authoritatively mar-shalled the assembly, while the ship's boat was called away. As the boat was about to proceed shoreward, a British Army officer suddenly appeared on the shore, and marched the prisoners away. The BBC next day announced that Taormina

158

had been captured singlehanded by a junior Army officer. There was no mention of the little *Cockchafer*, which on so many occasions had been shelled by mobile guns ashore, and had often been forced to beat a hasty and ignominious retreat.

It was on the night of 16 August 1943 that American troops entered Messina, followed by elements of 40 Royal Marine Commando the next morning, after their amphibious landing at Scaletta. Messina was being bombarded from across the straits, and there was no sign of the enemy, Axis troops having completed their evacuation some hours earlier. Operation HUSKY was over. The Allied objective had been accomplished. The Allies now stood before the gates of the Fortress of Europe, preparing for the next assault on the soft underbelly of the enemy.

11 Conclusion

The fall of Randazzo on 13 August had presaged the end of the fighting in Sicily. But Randazzo is 50 miles or more from Messina and the going hard. It was even harder for the advancing Allied troops than for the retreating forces, who by 14 August had broken all points of contact in their carefully planned withdrawal. The German reinforcements brought into the island in late July were not only for the purpose of putting up a strong defence but also to provide delaying action and effective cover for the regulated withdrawal that began on 11 August.

Mussolini had fallen from power on 25 July, to be succeeded by Marshal Badoglio, who declared Italy's intention of continuing the war on the side of the Germans. But the Germans had no illusions about the new Italian government's desire for an armistice. General Hube was given categorical instructions by Kesselring that the three superior German divisions already in the island must be extricated. To carry out this planned withdrawal, the German army was to retreat to successive defence lines. Each mile of withdrawal towards the apex of the triangle meant a contraction in the length of the defence line and the release of a proportionate number of German troops. Moreover it left less space for the converging Allied troops. Considerable demolition by the retiring troops frustrated the pursuers effectively. The evacuation extended over 5 days and 6 nights and was carried out so skilfully as to defeat the Allied armies in their late and abortive attempts at capturing men and weapons. The Allied air forces, however, were out in strength and claimed many successes. Nevertheless, with the conclusion of the German withdrawal at dawn on 17 August, General Hube could claim the salvation of 40,000 German troops, 10,000 vehicles, 47 tanks, 94 guns, and 17,000 tons of stores with which to supplement defensive action in the mainland of Italy.

In the Italian evacuation, which had been completed by noon on 16 August, 62,000 Italians had been transported to the mainland in an operation that Bragadin (*The Italian Navy in WWII*) says 'can be compared more than favourably with the British evacuation of Dunkirk'. He also remarks that in the course of this work fifteen landing barges, six minesweepers, and many small craft were lost, practically all through Allied air attacks. The figure 62,000 is hardly comparable with the 300,000 from Dunkirk, yet the audacity and effectiveness of the operation calls for admiration. Even more important is to enquire how it was allowed to happen.

The fortress commander at Messina controlled the batteries on both sides of the straits. In addition to having a large number of heavy and light anti-aircraft guns, his armament included powerful German mobile guns and robust Italian batteries of great strength and of long range on both sides of the straits. The distance across the straits varied from 2 to 5 miles and there were at least four Italian surface channels of communication and five German. The German point of view was that the narrow straits were easy to defend against air or sea attack. They were proved right, but it is still hard to understand why the Allies failed to make any concerted attempt to intercept the withdrawal of the Axis troops. There was certainly lack of cooperation on the part of the Allies during the latter part of the invasion for a number of reasons, the principal one being that the commanders were not together in one headquarters. Consideration was also being given to the next big operation.

The question as to why the successful Axis evacuation was not frustrated by the Allies, with their preponderance of sea

Ashore at last (IWM)

HMS Valiant *oiling destroyers; HMS* Formidable *in background* (IWM)

and air strength, has been much discussed. Roskill (*War at Sea*, Vol 3, part I) explains that the air commands primarily concerned were the North-West African Tactical Air Force under Air Vice-Marshal Coningham and the North-West African Strategic Air Force under General Doolittle. Both Coningham and Doolittle came under General Spaatz, with Tedder in overall command. It is clear that the evacuation problem was discussed by Doolittle and Coningham, and an agreement reached whereby heavy bombers of the Strategic Air Force would be available for the Tactical Air Force as soon as the evacuation began. The agreement was, however, amended a few days later by the imposition of a clause which said that transfer of task from Strategical to Tactical could only be effected after 12 hours' notice. The main German evacuation began on 11 August, but on such a small scale that Coningham reported that Tactical could handle the situation with its own resources and naval assistance. He also recommended that Strategic should be released from its commitment.

In the event, therefore, on the third day of the German evacuation, heavy bombers from Strategic were being employed in the bombing of Rome and other targets. Nor was there any sign of effectual naval assistance. Coningham had initially suggested a 'positive physical barrier, such as the Navy can provide'.

Though there appeared to be no coordinated plan either to subdue the powerful batteries in the straits or to produce any form of physical barrier, it is certain that the matter was raised by Admiral Cunningham's staff. Cunningham himself admits to paying insufficient attention to the matter. His staff were of the opinion that he paid attention all right, but could never forget the fate of some of the heavy ships sent in to bombard the heavy gun batteries in the Dardanelles in 1915. Without adequate air cover night and day, and because of the risk from mines and torpedoes, he was loth to commit ships for such purposes as bombardment unless it was certain that the benefits could be worth the risk.

Major-General G. Simonds (1 Canadian Division) wading ashore (**IWM**)

In a letter written on 28 November 1953 to a former member of his staff Cunningham said:

I am at the moment engaged in a long discussion by air mail with Morison, the US Naval historian. He wants to know why the Navy and the Air Force didn't stop the German divisions and some Italians getting back to Italy from Sicily. I don't think he realises the difficulty of stopping anyone trickling back over a journey of under twenty minutes. Still I have the sort of feeling that the Commanders-in-Chief never discussed it. (See S. W. C. Pack, *Cunningham the Commander*, p 259.)

The recipient of the above letter, a senior British Admiral, comments:

I believe, myself, that an attempt to prevent this traffic by surface forces would have been hazardous and costly in the extreme by day and ineffectual by night. Perhaps something might have been done less hazardously by round-the-clock air attacks, but I fancy that the air forces had many other calls to meet; moreover, we had not yet at that time developed dive-bombing to anything like the extent we did later on, following the example of our enemies.

It should not be concluded that nothing was done to stop the evacuation. On the very first night of the withdrawal, 11 August, three British Motor Torpedo Boats engaged six small craft with torpedoes and gunfire, and chased them into Messina. Other efforts were made on later nights, though little was achieved, and losses were suffered, HMS MTB 665 being sunk 15 August with all hands, and others being compelled to withdraw when fired on by batteries on both sides of the straits. The North-West African Air Force, Strategic (when available), as well as Tactical, attacked both by day and night, but the ferry traffic in the straits seemed to be immune from both high-level bombing and dive-bombing.

There was no intention of setting up base depots or permanent administrative centres in Sicily, as the campaign was expected to be too short to justify such establishments. Many administrative problems arose, however, as the armies swept northwards, capturing town after town, and these sometimes led to baffling as well as amusing situations often more difficult to resolve than some tactical point. Captain Rob Orme writes:

A memorable incident was the humbling of our quartermaster staff-captain in the HQ. He was a schoolmaster in private life and rather fancied himself as an Italian scholar. One day he received a letter from the Gestione Pozzi-neri complaining about sewage disposal. He had never heard of this body and thought the letter was from an individual with the usual illegible signature. He began his reply 'Egregio Signor Pozzi-Neri', in other words 'Dear Mr Cess-Pools'. It didn't go down at all well.

167

Lt-Col J. C. D. Scarlett, then a captain RA, describes some of the administrative problems:

> We disembarked at Syracuse on 14 July. I was promptly put on a 13cwt vehicle, accompanied by RAMC doctor, two drivers with sten guns, and told to get to Ragusa, which had just been taken by the Canadians. I was senior finance officer for the province of Ragusa and upon arrival, with the entire civilian population idle, had to get the people off the streets and fed, and the hospitals and such like had to be got going. The people begged for *assistenza*. There was no money as the Germans had instructed that it all be collected and then burnt. I got the local people to exchange what goods were available on the IOU system, until we received British Military Currency from England, and life became easier. I got most of the mayors of various places to cooperate. I was able to pump money into two adjacent asphalt mines and get several hundred men back to work and off *assistenza*, thus providing much needed asphalt for the runways in Allied airfields.

The individual pieces of equipment carried by each soldier on landing were a formidable burden. The load naturally varied according to task or assignment. Much of the stuff was irretrievably lost, and provision had to be made for replacement ashore; but this was understandably a slow process. Lance-Corporal Johnston lists his 'burden' as steel helmet with camouflage netting, gas mask, rolled ground sheet, field dressing, webbed equipment with pouches containing hand grenades, water bottle, entrenching tool, bayonet, small pack containing mess tin and emergency ration, a Bren gun and full 100 round circular magazine (for anti-aircraft fire).

Much was acquired by what was euphemistically referred to as 'borrowing', and there were various ways of getting essential articles. 'On the ridiculous side,' writes H. Ian Tait, 'I lost all my kit, and since I had reservations about sharing a razor I wrote to a friend in the USAF in Algeria. He got one to me by post before I was able to get one through "normal channels".'

Another event with a touch of the ironical is related by Brigadier J. D. Masters. He was troop leader with 50 Royal Tank Regiment (23 Armoured Brigade) and was attached to 5 Black Watch as tank landing officer. 'We landed,' he writes, 'at Cape Pachino without getting our feet wet. I have never forgotten the fine seamanship by the LCI captain. But the first casualty was the CO of 5 Black Watch, who was shot in the foot (accidentally) by one of his own soldiers. He was evacuated in the LCI that had just put him ashore.'

Masters refers to an order that called for the removal of identification marks from uniforms, for security reasons, and mentions 51 Highland Division, whose GOC was General Wimberley, 'a very Scots Scot', writes Masters, 'who was determined that the presence of the HD should not go unnoticed'.

> He had all his soldiers wear their shirts inside out before landing so as to comply with the order, and thus hide the divisional patch on the arm. Directly they got ashore they (the shirts) were all removed and put on the right way. Later Mount Etna had a sign on the summit which announced that it had been captured by 51 Highland Division, which was stretching the truth a little. This division became known as the Highway Decorators in the Eighth Army because of the proliferation of HD signs all over the country.

The story speaks well for the prestige and morale of the troops, which was generally high, and is borne out in the following letter written by J. W. Melville of 11 El Alamein RHA (HAC) Regiment.

'Our regiment was in support of 51 Highland Division,' writes Melville, 'I myself was Forward Observation Officer with one of their battalions, 5 Black Watch.' He describes how the brigade was drawn up as three sides of a large square, and Montgomery drove into the middle, standing up in a jeep. There were 1,500 of them, officers in front. All very formal at first. Then Monty said, 'Can't see your faces. Take your hats

off.' They did. Then he said, 'Gather round'. The men just pushed the officers forward and they were soon surrounding him. 'I was in England the other day,' said Monty, 'and I saw the Queen. *"Give my love to my Highlanders"*, she said.' This was greeted by tremendous cheering, and he was quickly off to address another brigade.

The Allies were lucky in having such able leaders as General Patton and General Montgomery in command of Seventh and Eighth Armies respectively. It is interesting to realise to what extent each of them possessed the qualities required for leadership: imagination, robustness, humanity, and opportunism. Although Eisenhower deprecated Patton's flamboyance, he regarded him as America's best fighting general. Of Montgomery, he speaks of his intelligence and refers to him as a very able dynamic type who loved the limelight. Perhaps it is the last characteristic that has limited public appreciation of Monty generally, but there is no doubt about the confidence his Eighth Army had in him, and the will to win that he inspired.

Casualties suffered by the navies, though not great when compared with army casualties, were by no means small. According to Morison, the US Navy lost 546 killed and 484 wounded. The Royal Navy lost 314 killed and 411 wounded. But these figures may not be altogether dependable. The armies continued a build-up throughout the campaign. Of a peak strength of 250,000, the Eighth Army lost nearly 5,000 killed or missing and 7,000 wounded, while the Seventh Army lost nearly 3,000 killed or missing and 6,000 wounded.

The stalemate and bloody fighting at Gerbini on the plains of Catania held up Monty long enough for Patton to win the race to Messina. There is a touch of irony in view of the plan

(opposite) (1 to r) *Generals Patton* (*US Seventh Army*), *de Guingand, Bradley, and Montgomery* (*British Eighth Army*)

that Patton was to take care of Monty's rear while Monty went forward to thrash the enemy as he had done from Alamein to Tunis.

Summarising, the HUSKY campaign remains an outstanding example of the value of sea and air power in an assault at some vulnerable point on the perimeter of hostile territory. In considering sea power, thought should be given to the crews of the merchant ships who, despite the possibility of additional hazard, carried out their tasks so efficiently and effectively. It is fortunate that ship losses were so relatively small, and this fact speaks well for the anti-submarine and anti-aircraft capabilities of the navies and air forces. Meanwhile skilful offensive action by British submarines inflicted losses in enemy shipping.

The most serious contingency was the sudden deterioration of weather a few hours before the assault, which caused for a while serious thoughts of a postponement. The judgement shown by the commanders was fully vindicated by events. The patient planning of elaborate detail culminated in a grand assembly of ships in the greatest seaborne force ever embarked at that time, and was crowned with success, for coast defences were surprised and subdued by supporting naval gunfire and all landing points were seized and consolidated in a matter of hours.

Operation HUSKY was unique in that several new designs of landing craft were first tried under warlike conditions and adverse weather. The new amphibious vehicle, the DUKW, proved its worth and made itself indispensable. Experience with this newcomer and others, such as the tank pontoon, was invaluable for the planning of future amphibious assaults.

HUSKY was notable for the absence of the enemy fleet, most of whose ships remained in port while Allied capital ships steamed at will, not only as covering forces, but on missions designed to mislead the enemy concerning the exact objective of the Allies. High among the deceptive measures was the planting of a dead body offshore, 'the man who never was', carrying papers marked top secret that indicated a spurious but specific objective for the coming assault.

The invasion and capture of Sicily in July and August 1943, so successfully performed, was the beginning of a number of assaults on the enemy territory, leading finally to unconditional surrender by the Germans in May 1945. The Italians would have liked to surrender after HUSKY but, unhappily, were compelled by the Germans to soldier on. They surrendered most of their warships, however, on 10 September 1943, and Cunningham, in what was one of his happiest moments, was then able to signal the Admiralty:

Be pleased to inform their Lordships that the Italian Fleet now lies at anchor beneath the guns of the fortress of Malta.

Appendix I

CHRONOLOGY OF EVENTS

Pre-HUSKY

1941

10 August	Churchill and Roosevelt sign Atlantic Charter
7 December	Japanese assault Pearl Harbour
22 December	First Washington Conference
25 December	British troops enter Benghazi

1942

28 January	British troops withdraw from Benghazi
	British Eighth Army stabilises at Gazala, west of Tobruk
February	Lull in desert warfare
	No British airfield now closer than 500 miles from Malta
April	Malta near collapse, receives carrier-borne Spitfires
June	British armour defeated Western Desert
21 June	British lose Tobruk
July	Rommel fails to break through at Alamein
	Anglo-American agreement for Allied landings NW Africa
August	Malta reinforced with carrier-borne Spitfires
	Relief of Malta
	Montgomery takes command of Eighth Army in Western Desert
	Eisenhower to command Allied forces
	Cunningham to command Allied Naval forces

August	Alexander appointed C-in-C Middle East
September	British preparing offensive in Western Desert
	Rommel preparing withdrawal
23 October	Battle of El Alamein opens
7 November	British break out at El Alamein
8 November	Allied landings in NW Africa
14 November	Eighth Army clears Axis forces from Cyrenaica

1943

14 January	Casablanca Conference
23 January	Eighth Army occupies Tripoli
20 March	Eighth Army move against Mareth Line
7 May	US forces capture Bizerta
	Tunis captured by British First Army
9 May	Fighting ends in Tunisia
13 May	Final HUSKY plan accepted by CCS
11 June	Pantelleria surrenders

During HUSKY

1943

5 July	British land forces make raids on Cretan airfields and withdraw successfully
10 July	British and US airborne troops land in Sicily
	US Seventh and British Eighth Armies, including Canadians, land on beaches
	British take Syracuse and Pachino
	Americans take Gela and Licata
11 July	US troops take Ragusa
13 July	Naval bombardment of Catania airfield
	British capture Augusta
14 July	Axis bomber attack north of Augusta repulsed by Allies
16 July	Canadians capture Caltagirone
17 July	Allied Military Government set up in Sicily: Alexander Military Governor
20 July	Canadians occupy Enna. Italians surrender en masse in West Sicily
21 July	US forces occupy Castelvetrano
	Naval bombardment of Crotone in Gulf of Taranto
	Canadians capture Leonforte
	British capture Gerbini airfield

22 July	45,000 Italians surrender in West Sicily
	Palermo captured by US forces
	US troops occupy Marsala and Trapani
25 July	US Seventh Army enters Termini
	Fall of Mussolini
28 July	Canadians capture Agira and US troops occupy Nicosia
30 July	Eighth Army takes Catenanuova
1 August	Allied forces start offensive against Axis line in NE Sicily
3 August	78 Division takes Centuripe, also Paterno and Misterbianco
	US forces capture Coronia
5 August	British troops enter Catania
7 August	Ustica Island (NW of Palermo) occupied
	British take Aderno
	Taormina bombarded by RN
9 August	British forces capture Guardia
12 August	Large-scale German evacuation of Sicily
15 August	Eighth Army captures Taormina
16 August	US forces enter Messina
	All Axis resistance in Sicily ends
	Italian mainland shelled from Messina
	Lipari Islands capitulate to US naval forces
18 August	General Badoglio broadcasts to the people of Italy.

Appendix II

SHIP LOSSES DURING ASSAULT

Date	Ship	Cause
10 July	Destroyer *Maddox*	Bombed
,,	Minesweeper *Sentinel*	Bombed
,,	S/M Chaser 694	Bombed and sunk at Palermo
,,	,, ,, 696	,, ,, ,, ,, ,,
,,	LST 158	Bombed
,,	,, 313	,,
,,	,, 318	Bombed during leapfrog landing east of Palermo
,,	LCI (L) 1	Bombed and sunk at Bizerta
,,	LCT (5) 154	Lost while in tow to Bizerta
,,	,, (,,) 311	,, ,, ,, ,, ,, ,,
11 July	Store Ship *Robert Rowan*	Bombed

EASTERN TASK FORCE

Date	Ship	Cause
3 July	LST 429	Fire
8 July	LCT 547	Foundered in heavy weather
10 July	LCP(R)	Fire from shell splinter
,,	Hospital Ship *Talamba*	Bombed
15 July	MGB 641	Sunk by Messina batteries
17 July	MTB 316	Sunk by shore battery
21 July	,, 288	Air attack in Augusta harbour
27 July	,, 63	Air attack at Syracuse
,,	LCT 353	,, ,, ,, ,,
11 August	Submarine *Parthian*	Missing

Date	*Ship*	*Cause*
15 August	MTB 665	Gunfire in Messina Straits
18 August	Submarine *Saracen*	Sunk off Bastia
,,	LCT 416	Explosion in LCT 416, Tripoli
,,	,, 301	,, ,, ,, ,, ,,

Bibliography

OFFICIAL HISTORIES OF WORLD WAR II

Bragadin, M. A. *Italian Navy* (USNI, Annapolis)
Howard, M. *Grand Strategy*, Vol IV (HMSO)
Molony, C. J. C. *The Mediterranean and Middle East*, Vol V (HMSO)
Morison, S. E. *United States Naval Operations*, Vol IX (Little, Brown)
Roskill, S. W. *The War At Sea*, Vols II, III (HMSO)

OTHER PUBLISHED WORKS

Ambrose, S. E. *The Supreme Commander* (Cassell, 1972)
Cole, H. *On Wings of Healing* (Blackwood, 1963)
Cunningham, A. B. *A Sailor's Odyssey* (Hutchinson, 1951)
de Guingand, F. *Operation Victory* (Hodder and Stoughton, 1947)
Dorling, T. *Western Mediterranean 1942-45* (Hodder and Stoughton, 1947)
Farago, L. *Patton: Ordeal and Triumph* (Barker, 1966)
Fergusson, B. *The Watery Maze* (Collins, 1961)
Montagu, E. *The Man Who Never Was* (Evans Bros, 1953)
Montgomery, B. *El Alamein to River Sangro* (Hutchinson, 1948)
Morison, S. E. *Two-Ocean War* (Little, Brown, 1963)
Pack, S. W. C. *Cunningham the Commander* (Batsford, 1974)
Reynolds, L. C. *Gunboat 658* (Kimber, 1955)
Vian, P. *Action This Day* (Muller, 1960)
Winterbotham, F. *Ultra Secret* (Weidenfeld & Nicolson, 1974)

Index

Aba, hospital ship, 120
Abdiel, HMS, 111
Abercrombie, monitor, 55, 80, 83
Acciaio, Italian submarine, 125
Aderno, 154–6, 158
Aegean sea, 24, 63
Agira, 148, 152, 156, 177
Agnew, Commodore W. G., 50, 110
Agnone, 138
Agrigento, 153
air cover, 30, 31, 36, 54, 61, 62, 64, 65, 68, 78, 79, 112, 117, 126, 165
Air Force:
    German, 17, 18, 24, 65, 66, 71, 83, 85, 118; Italian, 75, 109, 119, 120, 123; NW African, 61–4, 165, 167; Royal, 56, 62–6, 118, 127; US, 59, 84, 85, 88, 115, 168; Western Desert, 62, 113
Air Forces, Allied, 19, 27, 31, 52, 57, 60, 61, 65–70, 79, 85, 86, 115, 117, 118, 127, 133, 138, 153–5, 160, 161, 166, 167, 172; Axis, 24, 34, 57, 65, 68, 69, 78, 85, 97, 101, 115, 117, 119, 120, 125, 133
air superiority, 19, 34, 65, 66, 68, 78, 117–19, 134, 154, 165
Airborne Medical Society, 85
airborne operations, 31, 32, 37, 67–9, 74, 84–7, 92, 115, 125, 138–41
Aldworth, Major M., RM, 100, 147
Alexander, General Sir Harold, 21–3, 25, 31–5, 50, 67, 70, 150–3, 176
Allen, Major-General Terry, 40, 50, 78
Ambrosio, General, 68
amphibious operations, 16, 20, 30–2, 35, 43, 44, 52, 59–61, 63, 79, 127, 153–5, 158, 159, 172
Anapo, river, 41
Ancon, US HQ ship, 50, 77
Antwerp, HMS, 51, 89
armies, Allied, 113, 119, 144, 145, 153, 155–9, 160, 161; Axis, 15, 21, 23, 24,
31, 35, 67, 71, 72, 75, 119, 125, 133', 144, 145, 156, 158–61
Army, British, 34, 35, 50, 55, 58, 96, 117, 135, 138, 142, 145, 147–50
    1st, 23
    8th, 15, 22, 31, 32, 40, 51, 54, 74, 113, 115, 116, 125, 134, 135, 138, 141, 147, 150–2, 155, 156, 169, 171
    Airborne, 1st, 85, 87
    Argyll & Sutherland Highlanders, 103
    Black Watch, 5th, 169
    Brigade, 4th Armoured, 124, 138; 151st Infantry, 124, 138, 139; 231st, 51, 55, 90, 100, 148, 152, 156
    Devon Regiment, 100
    Division, 5th, 51, 86, 89, 93, 94, 135, 137, 138, 147, 156, 158; 50th, 51, 89, 135, 138, 141, 145, 147, 149, 158; 78th, 115, 125, 147, 152, 154–6, 158; Canadian 1st, 40, 46, 51, 53, 70, 81, 89, 92, 101, 102, 109, 110, 135, 145, 147, 148, 152, 154, 156, 168; Highland 51st, 51, 54, 72, 89, 91, 92, 94, 96, 102, 103, 110, 145–8, 152, 156, 158, 169, 171
    Dorset Regiment, 100, 101
    Durham Light Infantry, 138, 142
    Hampshire Regiment, 100, 101
    King's Own Yorkshire Light Infantry, 1st, 94
    Royal Army Medical Corps, 86
    Royal Artillery, 141, 144
    South Staffordshire regiment, 86
Army, German, 46, 68, 71, 72, 75, 80, 81, 97, 100, 106–8, 113, 115, 116, 135, 139, 142–56, 158–61, 168, 172
Army, Italian, 46, 56, 68, 71, 75, 80, 81, 83, 100, 101, 106, 114, 130, 141, 148, 150, 151, 154, 160, 161, 173
Army, US, 18, 35, 54, 55, 57, 73, 75, 78, 79, 81, 83, 88, 91, 115, 116, 135, 145, 154, 155, 158, 159, 171

7th, 22, 23, 31, 37, 40, 53, 59, 81, 89, 115, 125, 126, 135, 150, 151, 154, 155, 171

Division, 1st, 40, 78, 81, 153, 154; 3rd, 40, 41, 79, 81, 153, 158; 9th, 40, 154, 158; 45th, 40, 77, 81, 152, 153, 158; Airborne 82nd, 84, 85; Armoured 2nd, 40, 81

Arnold, General Henry, 15, 19

Ashbourne, Vice-Admiral Lord, 51, 55, 86, 90, 100, 101

Atlantic Ocean, 57, 62, 110

Augusta, 33, 41, 121–5, 135, 150, 166

Aurora, HMS, 50, 91, 110, 133

Avola, 34, 35, 41, 72, 89, 94, 96, 100, 138

Badoglio, Marshal, 160

Baker, B. A., 127

Berney-Ficklin, Major-General H. P. M., 41

Best, Rear-Admiral T. W., 45, 82

Biancavilla, 156

Birmingham, US cruiser, 50, 81

Biscari, 40

Biscayne, US HQ ship, 50, 75, 82

Blankney, HMS, 111

Boise, US cruiser, 50

bombardment, naval, 30, 32, 45, 47, 48, 56, 57, 67, 77, 79–82, 90, 91, 97, 99, 111, 117, 120, 126, 127, 132–4, 138, 153, 155, 158, 165, 172

Bon, Cape, 47, 57, 110

Bonzo, Italian submarine, 123

Bragadin, M. A., 161

BRIMSTONE, Operation, 18, 20, 25

British Joint Staff Mission, 16, 18

Broadhurst, Air Vice-Marshal, 22, 62, 144

Brolo, 158

Brooke, General Sir Alan, 16, 19, 20

Brooklyn, US cruiser, 50, 81

Buccheri, 107, 147

Bullen, Lieut, 72

Bulolo, HMS, 51, 121

Buoys, sonic, 43, 91

Butt, Captain R. D., RN, 93, 97

Calabria, 134

Caltagirone, 147

Cameron, Captain I. C., 106

Campobello, 79

Campofelice, 153

Carlentini, 142

Carlisle, HMS, 121–3

Carriers, aircraft; *see also under* individual names

Casablanca, 15, 17, 18, 21, 31, 62

Cassibile, 41, 89, 97, 99, 100

Castelvetrano, 24, 31

casualties; *see* losses

Catania, 24, 30, 33, 36, 41, 71, 91, 108, 115, 124, 125, 132, 134, 135, 141–5, 147, 149–52, 155, 156, 171

Catenanuva, 147

Cavour, class battleships, 69

Centuripe, 154–6

Cesaro, 154

Chiefs of Staff, British, 16–18, 20

Chiefs of Staff, Combined, 15, 16, 19, 21, 35, 57

Chiefs of Staff, Joint, 15,

Chiefs of Staff, US, 15, 16, 18, 20

Churchill, Winston, 15, 16, 19–21, 25, 37, 68

City of Venice, MT store ship, 54, 110, 145

Clarkson, Cdr R. A., RN, 121

Cleopatra, HMS, 50, 110, 133

Cockchafer, HMS, 158, 159

Colin P. Kelly, US MT store ship, 69

Collier, C., 69

Colombo, HMS, 80

Comiso, 31, 34, 40

Commandos, 99, 124, 127, 138, 141, 155, 159

communications, 19, 20, 31, 56, 63, 65, 77, 80, 82, 126, 127

Coningham, Air Marshal Arthur, 61, 165

Conolly, Rear-Admiral, 50, 75, 82, 83

Corleone, 153

Corniche road, 155

Corsica, 19, 25

Crete, 24, 25, 65, 66, 85, 134

Croxton, Lieut, 72

Cruiser Squadron, 12th, 50

Cruiser Squadron, 15th, 48

Cunningham, Admiral of the Fleet Sir Andrew, 20–2, 32–6, 47, 48, 56, 57, 59, 60, 65, 67, 73, 74, 80, 84, 87, 112, 133, 134, 154, 155, 165, 166, 173

Cygnet, HMS, 70

Daniell, Lieut A., RN, 91

Davidson, Rear-Admiral, USN, 153, 154, 158

Dempsey, Lieut-General, 31, 33

Derna, 54

Destroyer Flotilla, 6th, 48; 19th, 48; 21st, 92

Devis, MT ship, 54, 110

Dido, HMS, 50, 110

Dieppe, 83

Dill, Field-Marshal Sir John, 16, 18

Dittaino river, 147

Djidjelli, 82
Doolittle, Major-General James, 61, 165
Dorsetshire, hospital ship, 129
Douglas, Air Chief Marshal Sir William Sholto, 62, 65
Duca d'Aosta, Italian cruiser, 154
Duchess of Bedford (LSI), 90, 97
DUKWs, 44, 107, 112, 172

Echo, HMS, 125
Eddy, Major-General, 40
Eisenhower, General Dwight D., 18, 21–3, 32, 33–5, 57, 59, 67, 79, 81, 171
El Alamein, 15, 172
Eldridge, Captain J. C. E., RASC, 97
Empedocle, 81, 153
England, Rear-Admiral Hugh T., 110
Erebus, HMS, 90, 124, 133
Eskimo, HMS, 91, 99, 121
Etna, Mount, 94, 100, 107, 134, 145, 151, 152, 156, 158, 169
Euryalus, HMS, 50, 110, 134
evacuation, 150, 154–6, 158–61, 165–7
Evans, Richard, 112
Evelegh, Major-General, 41, 156

Farello airfield, 85
Fergusson, Bernard, 44
Field Ambulance, 181st (Air Landing), 86
Fleet Air Arm, 52, 65
fleet in being, 24, 119
Flores, Dutch gunboat, 101
Flutto, Italian submarine, 124
Formidable, HMS, 48, 52, 62, 64, 134
Frankcom, Captain C., 46

Gaffey, Major-General, 40
Gairdner, Major-General, 31
Garibaldi, Italian cruiser, 154
Gartside, Surgeon-Captain V., 158
Gela, 24, 30, 34, 40, 69, 75, 77–81, 83–5, 89, 135
Gerbini, 24, 31, 107, 108, 134, 135, 146, 148, 150, 151, 171
Gibraltar, 22, 24, 59, 64, 70, 131
Glennon, US destroyer, 80
Grand Harbour, Malta, 59
Grande bridge, 41
Guzzoni, General, 68, 71, 72, 75

Hall, Rear-Admiral, 50, 76, 78, 81
Harcourt, Rear-Admiral, 48, 124, 131
Hesketh, S., 127
Hewitt, Vice-Admiral Henry, USN, 22, 50, 59, 62, 74, 77, 88, 89, 154
Hickey, Colonel T. J., USAAF, 22, 61

Hilary, HMS, 51, 70, 92, 109, 111
Hitler, Adolf, 67, 71, 150
Hopkinson, Major-General G. F., 87
Howe, HMS, 48, 91, 133
Hube, General, 150, 160, 161

Iberian peninsula, 23
Ilex, HMS, 125
Inconstant, HMS, 123
Indomitable, HMS, 48, 52, 62, 133, 134
Italians, 67, 68, 101, 141
Italy, 18–20, 23, 63, 67, 68, 72, 119, 149, 160, 161, 166

Johnston, Lance-Corporal, 168

Keren (LSI), 51, 56, 87, 90, 100, 101
Kesselring, Marshal, 68, 71, 150, 160
Keyes, Admiral Sir Roger, 57
King, Admiral E. J., USN, 15, 18
King George V, HMS, 48, 91, 133
Kirk, Rear-Admiral Alan, 50, 66, 77, 78
Kirkman, Major-General S. C., 41, 145

Laforey, HMS, 91
Lampedusa, 57
landing craft, 16–18, 24, 34, 41, 43–6, 48, 52, 56, 57, 59, 69, 73, 74, 76, 77, 79, 80, 86, 89, 90, 92–7, 99–103, 106–109, 111–13, 115–18, 122, 129, 133, 139, 153, 161, 169, 172
Langford-Sainsbury, Air Vice-Marshal T. A., 62, 65
Largs (LSI), 51, 54, 102
Lathbury, Brigadier Gerald, 141
Laycock, Brigadier R. E., 70
Leese, Lt-General Sir Oliver, 40
Lentini, 124, 135, 138, 142, 149
Leonforte, 151, 152, 156
Licata, 40, 75, 79, 81–5, 89, 153
Linguaglossa, 158
Littorio, Italian battleship, 69
Lloyd, Air Marshal Sir Hugh, 61, 64
Lloyd, Captain, 72
Lombard-Hobson, Lieut, S. R., RN, 98
Lloyd, Air Marshal Sir Hugh, 61, 64
Lookout, HMS, 91
Losses, Allies', 54, 64, 66, 78, 80, 83, 85–7, 92, 102, 110, 117, 118, 120–3, 129, 131, 133, 143, 145–7, 151, 153, 167, 171, 172, 178, 179
Loyal, HMS, 91
Luck, Miss Mary, 129

McGrigor, Rear-Admiral R. R., 51, 57, 89, 102, 125, 155

McPherson, Lieut B. D., RNR, 83
Maddox, US destroyer, 78, 80
Mafia, 113, 115, 116
Malati bridge, 135, 138
Malta, 27, 31, 40, 48, 51, 54, 57, 59, 61, 64, 65, 69, 70, 73, 74, 84, 85, 89–91, 102, 110–14, 116, 123, 125, 129, 134, 173
'Man who never was,' the, 25, 172
Marsala, 81, 91
Marshall, General George, 15, 18, 19
Martin, Major-General, 139
Marzamemi, 41, 51, 55, 90, 100, 101
Massiera Parlato, 148, 149
Masters, Brigadier J. D., 169
Mauritius, HMS, 48, 91, 120
Mazzara, 27, 30
medical services, 55, 85, 86, 121, 129–31
Mediterranean Sea, 17–20, 22, 24, 32, 34, 47, 50, 53, 54, 57, 64–7, 70, 79, 86, 98, 99, 110, 119, 131
Mediterranean strategy, 17–20
Melville, J. W., 169
Messina, 71, 72, 149–51, 153, 155, 159, 160, 161, 167, 171
Messina, Straits of, 23, 27, 72, 123, 133, 158, 159, 161, 165, 167
Middleton, Major-General T. C., 40, 50, 77, 153
Milo, 31
MINCEMEAT, Operation, 25, 26, 68, 71
mines and minefields, 56, 72, 77, 78, 99, 101, 120, 129, 142, 143, 153, 156, 165
minesweeping, 77, 92, 102, 111, 120, 123, 133, 143, 161
Misterbianco, 156
Mitchener, B. O., 99
Monarch of Bermuda (LSI), 90
Monrovia, US HQ ship, 50, 53, 59, 77
Montagu, Ewen, 75
Montgomery, General Sir Bernard, 15, 22, 31, 32, 33–5, 40, 51, 71, 117, 125, 135, 141, 145–7, 151, 152, 155, 156, 169, 171, 172
morale, 94, 117, 131, 169, 171
Morison, Rear-Admiral S. E., 33, 62, 74, 75, 154, 166, 171
Mountbatten, Lord Louis, 16, 20, 46, 70, 81
Mulinello, river, 41
Mulleneux, Cdr H. H. H., 45
Murro di Porco, 94
Mussolini, Benito, 57, 67, 68, 119, 150, 160

Naval Co-operation Group RAF, 63, 64, 65
Navies:

Allied, 48, 52, 59, 60, 62, 80, 88, 117, 119, 123, 125, 138, 165, 171, 172; Axis, 68; Belgian, 52; Dutch, 52; Greek, 52; Italian, 24, 47, 69, 94, 119, 120, 123, 173; Norwegian, 52; Polish, 52; Royal, 48, 56, 83, 88, 89, 119, 155, 167, 171, 172; US, 48, 55, 62, 77, 88, 153, 154, 171.
Negro, Cape, 69
Nelson, HMS, 48, 133
Nelson, Vice-Admiral Viscount, 60
Nereide, Italian submarine, 125
Newfoundland, HMS, 48, 91, 133, 138
Nicosia, 151, 153, 156
night operations, 21, 32, 41–4, 48, 69, 74, 76, 77, 82, 85–8, 90–2, 94–6, 98–101, 103, 106, 111, 113, 118, 142, 146, 148, 167
Niscemi, 84
Noto, 127, 147
Nubian, HMS, 91

Orion, HMS, 48, 91
Orme, Captain Rob, 167
Otranto, (LSI) 56, 90, 100

Pachino, 34, 35, 40, 51, 81, 89–91, 101, 102, 110, 169
Palazzolo, 147
Palermo, 24, 27, 30, 31, 34–6, 71, 81, 115, 153–5
Pantelleria, 57, 64, 86
parachute troops, 31, 32, 37, 67–9, 74, 83–7, 92, 115, 125, 139, 141, 145, 146
Parberry, Major P., RA, 141
Park, Air Vice-Marshal Sir Keith, 12, 65
Parry, Admiral C. R. L., 92
Passero, Cape, 55, 98, 108, 138
Paterno, 152, 156
Patience, Captain A., 120
Patton, Lt-General George, 22, 31, 33, 40, 50, 53, 59, 62, 81, 126, 135, 150–3, 155, 171, 172
Pearson, Colonel Alistair, 139
Penelope, HMS, 50, 91, 110, 133
Petralia, 153
Philadelphia, US cruiser, 50, 158
photography, 24, 30, 56, 67, 69, 72, 127, 129
Picken, John, 120
Ponte Grande, 86
Ponte Olivo, 24, 31, 34, 40, 80, 81
pontoons, portable, 44
Portal, Air Chief Marshal Sir Charles, 16, 19, 20
Portopalo, 51, 89, 91, 106

Pound, Admiral of the Fleet Sir Dudley, 16, 19, 20
Pozzallo, 35
Price, Captain D. L. C., RA, 141
Pridham, Lieut Tony, 138
Primosole bridge, 41, 135, 138, 139, 141, 145, 151
Princess Beatrix (LSI), 102
Prins Albert (LSI), 124, 138
Puckeridge, HMS, 111
Punta Castellazo, 40
Punta di Formiche, 40, 109
Punta Murazzo, 124

Queen Emma (LSI), 102
Queen Mary, liner, 99
Quill, Colonel H., RM, 72

radar, 45, 68, 123, 127
radio, 77, 97, 113, 114, 127
Ragusa, 40, 168
Ramacca, 147
Ramsay, Admiral Sir Bertram, 22, 31, 33, 50, 59, 89, 117, 118, 121, 125, 154
Randazzo, 151, 153, 155, 156, 158, 160
Regalbuto, 148, 153, 154, 156
Regolo, Italian cruiser, 133
Reina del Pacifico (LSI), 90, 93, 94, 96
rescue, air-sea, 70
Rigby-Jones, Captain G., 86
Roberts, HMS, 90, 111, 126, 133, 155
rockets, 44, 45, 82, 117
Rockwood, HMS, 98, 99
Rodd, Commander, 72
Rodney, HMS, 48, 133
Rommel, Field-Marshal E., 23
Roosevelt, President F. D., 15, 16, 19, 21
Roskill, S. W., 66, 165
Rosolini, 101
ROUND-UP, Operation, 18–20
Royal Marines, 89, 109, 113, 147, 155, 159
Royal Scotsman (LSI), 102
Royal Ulsterman (LSI), 102, 103
Russia, 17, 19–21, 68

Safari, HM submarine, 74
Saint Essylt, MT store ship, 54, 110, 145
Samuel Chase, US HQ ship, 50, 76
S. Agata, 153, 154, 158
S. Caterina, 153
San Stefano, 145, 153, 158
Sardinia, 18–21, 24, 25, 63, 67
Saul, Air Vice-Marshal R. E., 62
Savannah, US cruiser, 50, 80

Scaletta, 155, 159
Scarlett, Lt-Colonel J. C. D., RA, 168
Schmalz, Colonel, 135, 138
Sciacca, 27, 30, 31, 34
Scoglitti, 40, 77, 81, 85, 89, 153
Seaham, HMS, 123
Seal, Major G. H., 139
Searl, Group Captain F. H. L., 113, 114
security, 23–6, 33, 42, 48, 55, 63, 74, 75, 94, 99, 132, 133, 169, 172, 173
Senior, Brigadier R. H., 142
Seraph, HM submarine, 74
Shahjehan, MT ship, 54
Shakespeare, HM submarine, 74
'ship to shore', 41, 51
'shore to shore', 41, 51, 100, 103
Sicily, 18–25, 27, 30, 32, 36, 37, 48, 53, 57, 62–71, 75, 81, 84, 89, 91, 93, 97–100, 110, 113, 116, 132, 134, 150–2, 154, 158, 160, 166, 167, 173
Simeto, river, 41, 135, 138, 142, 145
Simonds, Major-General G. G., 40, 70
Sirius, HMS, 50, 116
smokescreens, 117, 125
Soemba, Dutch gunboat, 101
Solomon, Lieut, 72
Spaatz, Lt-General Carl, 61, 64, 165
Spain, 18, 25
Stalin, 17
Stay, R. F., 45
Sterne, Geoffrey, 115
Stimson, Secretary, 22
Strathnaver (LSI), 56, 90, 100, 101
submarines, 16, 19, 20, 24, 41, 43, 50, 52, 54, 56, 70, 74, 75, 77, 110, 123–5, 133, 172
surrender, unconditional, 20, 173
Swanson, US destroyer, 79
Syracuse, 30, 31, 33, 41, 69, 84, 86, 89, 93, 94, 97, 117, 120–5, 127, 135, 141, 154, 168

Tait, H. Ian, 103, 146, 168
Talamba, hospital ship, 117, 121, 129
tanks, 30, 44, 45, 51, 57, 79–81, 90, 101, 102, 109, 138, 146–9, 155, 161
Taormina, 91, 126, 143, 158
Taranto, 69, 133
Tartar, HMS, 91
Task Forces:
  Eastern, 21, 22, 32, 34, 48, 50, 62, 66, 80, 89, 91, 117, 125; Western, 21, 22, 32, 34, 48, 50, 53, 55, 59, 61, 66, 74, 80, 81, 88, 89, 125, 126
Task Group, 88, US, 153
Tedder, Air Chief Marshal Sir Arthur, 21, 22, 31–4, 35, 61, 63, 66, 165
Termini, 153

Tetcott, HMS, 124
Timothy Pickering, US MT ship, 131
Tollet, Rev D., 100
TORCH, Operation, 16, 59, 62, 64
torpedoes, 43, 59, 110, 123, 133, 145, 165, 167
training, 17, 24, 32, 42, 55–7, 59, 82, 93, 99
Trapani, 81, 91, 133
Troina, 154, 156
Troubridge, Rear-Admiral T. H., 51, 89, 120, 121, 125
Truscott, Major-General L. K., 40, 50, 79, 81, 153
Tunis, 40, 53, 56, 84, 172
Tunisia, 18, 20, 21, 23, 27, 31, 35, 41, 50, 53, 56, 63, 65, 85, 139, 145
Tweedie, Squadron-Leader, 127

Uganda, HMS, 48, 59, 91, 120
Ulster Monarch (LSI), 124
ULTRA, German cypher, 24, 70, 71, 113, 116
Unison, HM submarine, 91, 93
United States of America, 16, 23, 40, 50, 53, 57, 115, 116

Unrivalled, HM submarine, 92, 93
Unruffled, HM submarine, 93
Unruly, HM submarine, 125
Urquhart, Brigadier R. E., 41

Valiant, HMS, 48, 134
Vian, Rear-Admiral Sir Philip, 57, 70, 89, 92, 109, 110, 125
Vizzini, 147

Warspite, HMS, 48, 97, 134
Washington, 15, 16, 23, 25, 34
weather influence, 21, 56, 67, 79, 82–7, 89, 91–4, 97, 98, 100, 102, 103, 106, 110, 111, 133, 149, 172
Whimbrel, HMS, 70
Whitfield, John, RE, 107, 108
Willis, Vice-Admiral Sir Algernon, 48
Wimberley, Major-General D. N., 40, 169
Winchester Castle (LSI), 90
Winterbotham, Group Captain F., 70

Zoe, US destroyer, 79

OPERATION
HUSKY
The Allied Invasion of Sicily
S W C Pack

The Allied objectives of 'Husky', the first
strike at the enemy in his own land, were
clear: to make the Mediterranean safe for
shipping; to divert enemy strength from
Russia; and to knock Italy out of the war.
It was a massive combined operation, first
seriously planned only six months before
it took place, and by senior commanders
in headquarters widely dispersed, from
Washington and London to Algiers and
Cairo. There were ten Allied divisions and
additional units of airborne forces.

The first landings were made on 10
July, 1943 and by 16 August all Axis resistance ceased. Two days later Italy
capitulated. The operation has been
recounted as part of the history of World
War II but now Captain Pack provides in
narrative form a detailed account of it as
a whole, never overlooking the personal
experiences of individual officers and
other ranks.

The order of the day was that the battle
must go on, whatever the weather, whatever
the cost. The weather, for instance,
deteriorated to such a degree that there
were serious thoughts of postponement,
and men had to land in the night in water
too deep for wading. But the operation
went on to secure the essential foothold
for the invasion of the Italian mainland.